The

GREATEST STORIES
NEVER TOLD

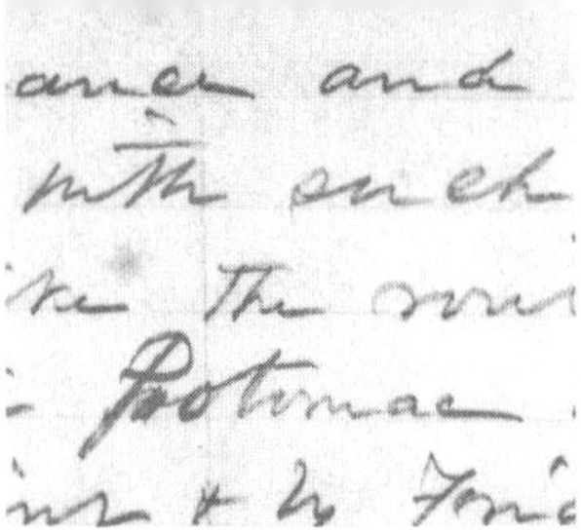

by Rick Beyer

HarperResource

An Imprint of HarperCollins*Publishers*

 **HISTORY** *Presents*

The

GREATEST STORIES
NEVER TOLD

100 *Tales from History to Astonish, Bewilder & Stupefy*

HarperCollins books may be purchased for educational, business, or sales promotional use. For information, please write: Special Markets Department, HarperCollins Publishers Inc., 10 East 53rd Street, New York, NY 10022.

Design by Judith Stagnitto Abbate / Abbate Design

Printed on acid-free paper

Library of Congress Cataloging-in-Publication Data is available upon request.

ISBN 0-06-001401-6

09 ˙ / RRD   40 39 38 37 36 35 34

For my dad

H istory is filled with unpredictable people and unbelievable stories. ■ Consider: The Pilgrims landed in Plymouth because they ran out of beer. Annie Oakley almost shot Kaiser Wilhelm before World War I. Three cigars changed the course of the Civil War. The stethoscope was invented by a modest French doctor reluctant to put his ear to a female patient's bosom. An Italian priest perfected the first practical fax machine in 1863. Teddy Roosevelt is the father of football's forward pass. And believe it or not, actress Hedy Lamarr not only appeared in the movies' first nude scene, but also later patented an idea that formed the basis for cell phone encryption. As Dave Barry would say: "I am not making this up."

Historian David McCullough points out, "There is no such thing as the past." History is created in the present, by living, breathing people. They do what they do under deadline, on the fly, in the heat of anger, or sometimes completely by accident. Which is precisely why the history they make can be so surprising, compelling, and utterly entertaining. History isn't always made by great armies colliding or great civilizations falling. Sometimes it is made when a chauffeur takes a wrong turn, a scientist forgets to clean up his lab, or a drunken soldier gets a bit rowdy. That's the kind of history you'll find in these pages.

This book had its genesis when THE HISTORY CHANNEL® asked me to create a series of "history minutes" marking the millennium. When *Timelab 2000*® hit the air, the response was overwhelmingly positive. The series generated glowing e-mails from teachers, news anchors, ministers, mothers, and high school students. People couldn't seem to get enough of the special brand of history those minutes contained.

So, for everyone who loves stories like these as much as I do, here's a whole book full: one hundred tales from history to astonish, bewilder, and stupefy. Stories so good they cry out to be told. Some originally appeared on THE HISTORY CHANNEL; others I saved just for this book. Some are emotional, some sheer fun; others simply defy belief. My goal has been to make each story jump out and grab you the same way it first grabbed me. I'll leave it to you to judge whether that effort succeeded.

Are they truly "the greatest stories never told"? Quite obviously, they've all been told *someplace,* otherwise I couldn't have found them. But yesterday's headline is today's forgotten gem. Stories buried deep in the pages of a heavy tome take on a new life when considered on their own. Chances are you will find most of these pieces quite astonishing to hear—and to see. The stories are accompanied by more than two hundred illustrations, gathered from libraries, archives, and private collections the world over. They help bring history to life in a way words alone simply cannot.

"History would be a wonderful thing," said Leo Tolstoy, "if only it were true." Ascertaining the veracity of these stories involved quite a bit of detective work. Sometimes a wonderful tale seemed too good to be true, and it was. A good example is the story of how Silly Putty traveled to the moon on *Apollo 8*. You'll find that story in at least fifty websites and several books. Calls to two of the *Apollo 8* astronauts, however, as well as to Binney & Smith, makers of Silly Putty, confirmed that it is just an urban legend. To screen out oft-repeated fallacies and legends—urban or otherwise—every story has been painstakingly researched, then reviewed by an historian.

So feel free to pass them along to others. Go ahead, trot them out at cocktail parties or read them to your children. Don't hesitate to share your surprise and amusement and awe with friends and family. Bizarre as they may seem, they are as true as I know how to make them.

Winston Churchill once said that writing a book is an adventure. "To begin with it is a toy and an amusement. Then it becomes a mistress, then it becomes a master, then it becomes a tyrant. The last phase is that just as you are about to be reconciled to your servitude, you kill the monster and fling him to the public." I am now ready to fling this one to you. I hope reading it will prove to be an adventure of its own, and that you will be delighted by the discoveries awaiting you in the pages that follow. ■

THE MEN WHO STOLE TIME

We've all heard of public corruption. But stealing time itself?

The early Romans used the moon as a measure of the months. That led to a twelve-month year that came up short, with only 355 days. To keep the seasons straight, the custom of occasionally adding extra weeks and months began. But the potential for mischief was too great a temptation. Corrupt public officials began to manipulate the calendar to prolong their terms in office and shorten the terms of hated rivals. In essence they were stealing time to further their own political purposes.

By 46 B.C., the Roman year was more than two months off. That's when Julius Caesar took charge. He mandated a new solar calendar, making the year 365 days long. He changed New Year's Day from March 1 to January 1, and added an extra day every four years. Opponents grumbled that Caesar, not content with ruling the earth, was now trying to command the heavens above.

To bring the calendar back on track, Caesar added two extra months to the year 46 B.C.—sticking them in between November and December. He also squeezed in an extra three weeks between February and March. The result was a year such as no one had ever seen before—445 days long. In Rome this forever became known as the "year of confusion," even though, as Caesar himself was quick to point out, it was actually the year the confusion came to an end.

Caesar might never have cleaned up the calendar if it hadn't been for his most famous lover: the beguiling Cleopatra, portrayed here by the famed nineteenth-century actress Lillie Langtry. Cleopatra introduced Caesar to the Egyptian astronomer Sosigenes, who explained the idea of a calendar based on the sun, then traveled to Rome to help Caesar put it into effect.

In the Roman calendar, days were divided into 12 hours of light and 12 hours of darkness. So a daytime "hour" on a long summer day might be the equivalent of an hour and 15 minutes today, whereas an hour on a winter day might be as short as 45 minutes.

THE OLYMPICS: CANCELED

The day the games were shut down for religious reasons.

In ancient Greece, the Olympic Games were held every four years in tribute to the god Zeus. They began in 776 B.C. and continued for more than a thousand years. They were male-only affairs—women weren't allowed to compete, or even to watch. These competitions were considered so important that when the games were held, trade was suspended and wars were postponed. Even after the Romans conquered Greece, the games continued.

But in 394 A.D. the Roman emperor Theodosius put a stop to the games. Why? After converting to Christianity a decade before, Theodosius had become a religious zealot determined to stamp out all pagan worship. He considered the games to be a scandalous glorification of the ancient Greek gods. So he ended them for all time—or so he thought.

For the next fifteen hundred years, the Olympics were but a distant memory. In 1892 a twenty-seven-year-old French baron named Pierre de Coubertin proposed reviving the Olympic ideal. The initial response from athletic officials: a big yawn. But Coubertin's single-minded devotion eventually carried the day. So it was that in 1896 the modern Olympics were born and, after a span of more than a millennium, once again brought the world together in sport.

One of Coubertin's underlying motives in launching the Olympic movement was to improve the physical fitness of the French, so that his countrymen would be better prepared in the event of war with Germany. He also considered sports to be a great source of moral energy.

The first modern Olympiad—in Athens, Greece—featured just 311 athletes from thirteen nations, a far cry from the ten thousand that gather at the Olympics today. All of the athletes at those first games were men: just as in ancient times, women weren't allowed to compete. (That changed with the next Olympics.) The United States led all nations, with eleven gold medals.

KIDNAPPED

From slavery to sainthood.

In the fading days of the Roman Empire, a sixteen-year-old boy was abducted into slavery by savages outside the border of the civilized world. They took him to a remote land beyond the sea, where he labored under the harshest conditions.

The boy had never been very religious, but in desperation he began to pray to God every day that he might survive his horrible ordeal. After more than five years in bondage, he was able to escape. He walked two hundred miles to a seaport, where he found passage on a ship that carried him away. Eventually he returned home to joyous parents who begged him never to leave again.

But night after night he was tormented by dreams and visions. Voices beckoned. They told him he must return to the land of his kidnappers and bring the word of Christ into this savage land.

And that's exactly what he did.

The boy lived in what is now England. His kidnappers were Celtic tribesman from across the water—Ireland. And that's how a young Briton named Patricius grew into an old Irishman named Patrick. Saint Patrick, to be exact.

The patron saint of Ireland: an Englishman by birth.

Saint Patrick did not drive the snakes out of Ireland. In truth, the island nation is too cold for snakes. That particular legend is believed to be a metaphor for Patrick's spectacular success in driving the idol-worshiping Druid religion out of Ireland and converting almost the entire population to Christianity.

> ❝ WE BEG YOU TO COME
> AND WALK AMONG US
> ONCE MORE. ❞

—VOX HIBERNIAE, "THE VOICE OF THE
IRISH," SPEAKING TO PATRICIUS IN
HIS DREAMS

The slave business flourished in Ireland for centuries before Patrick's arrival on the scene. Celtic raiding parties would kidnap hundreds of people at a time. Boys were brought back to be sheepherders and girls to be sex slaves. One of Patrick's accomplishments was to largely put an end to this slave trade.

WATER WORLD

The barbarians we have to thank for the birth of a legendary city.

Rape and pillage. Houses torched, crops stolen, and hasty graves for bloody corpses. This was the legacy of Attila's Huns, sweeping across northern Italy and wreaking havoc and destruction on the remnants of the Roman Empire. But they unintentionally left another, more positive legacy as well.

Refugees fled from burning cities, desperate to find safe refuge. Some literally took to the swamps, finding sanctuary in a desolate group of islands in a marshy lagoon off the northern Adriatic. When the Huns were followed by other invading tribes, more Roman citizens streamed to the swamps to avoid the carnage and destruction on the mainland.

Over the next few centuries they transformed the inhospitable surroundings into an architectural wonder: Venice! With more than four hundred bridges and almost two hundred canals, it became a center of trade and a seafaring

power. Built out of misfortune, Venice eventually turned into one of the richest and most beautiful cities in the world.

Harsh necessity can be the mother of glorious invention.

The city of Venice was built on 118 islands two and a half miles from the mainland. Its streets are a precarious few inches above sea level, and are currently sinking at a frightening level: about one inch every ten years. Efforts are under way to protect the city from being overcome by the ocean.

The gondolas that dot the waterways of Venice have been around for at least a thousand years, with the first known mention of them coming in 1094. They evolved over the centuries, and it wasn't until the 1700s that they finally assumed the form familiar today. These gondoliers were photographed in 1869.

66 **YOU LIVE LIKE SEA BIRDS.** 99

—ROMAN STATESMAN CASSIODORUS, IN A LETTER TO VENETIANS, CIRCA 537

THE DEATH OF ATTILA

A warrior poised to conquer the world, until marriage proved his undoing.

Attila the Hun. Even today the name conjures up images of pillage and destruction. King of the Huns for twenty years, he commanded an army of half a million men, made all of Europe tremble, and threatened to capture Rome itself.

But the terrifying Attila died before he completed his conquest of the civilized world, and it wasn't on the battlefield. It was on his wedding night.

In the year 453, Attila took a new wife: a young girl named Ildico, renowned for her beauty. After a night of drunken revelry in celebration of the wedding, he retired with his bride to the bedchamber, where he promptly passed out on his back.

The following day servants became alarmed when Attila didn't rise at the normal time. After their shouts failed to wake him, they knocked down the door. Inside they found the body of their chieftain sprawled out on the bed beside his weeping bride.

Was he the victim of murder at the hands of his new wife? Not at all. It seems that for all his power and might, the great conqueror had a weakness—he suffered from chronic nosebleeds. One apparently came upon him in his drunken state, and he choked to death.

So it was that one of history's most fearsome warriors died not from a bloody wound but from a bloody nose.

Shortly before he died, Attila was bearing down on Rome with a great army. But Pope Leo I came out to meet with Attila, and convinced him to turn away. People thought it was a miracle, but actually Attila was low on supplies. Two years after Attila's death, another barbarian tribe sacked the city. It was an event so frightening that it burned the name of the attackers into our vocabulary. They were called…the Vandals.

At Attila's funeral, his body was laid out in a silk tent, and horsemen rode in circles around it. Many of his followers gashed their faces so that they would weep blood at his death. His burial party was murdered so that his grave might never be found.

THE MAN WHO DIDN'T DISCOVER AMERICA

Bjarni Herjulfson could have become one of the most famous explorers in history, if only he'd gotten out of his boat!

Bjarni was lost at sea. On his way to Greenland, fierce autumn storms had buffeted his ship for days. They had blown him so far off course that he had no idea where he was. Once the weather cleared, he was relieved to see land. But this land looked totally unfamiliar. It had no mountains or glaciers as Greenland did, only small hills and forests. Bjarni didn't know it, but he had crossed the Atlantic and sailed to what is now Canada.

His crew begged him to land. If only he had the spirit of a Christopher Columbus, this might have been a defining moment in exploration. But Bjarni was intent on going home, not going down in history. So without even leaving his boat, he turned right around and headed out to sea. He and his crew finally made it to Greenland a week later.

Years afterward, he told his tale of adventure to a friend, who decided to retrace Bjarni's course. And so it was that Leif Eriksson staked his claim as the first European to walk on the American continent.

Bjarni went down in history as the man whose curiosity did *not* get the better of him.

Not only did Leif Eriksson question Bjarni closely about his journey—he actually purchased Bjarni's ship and used it for his own trip.

> 66 **MANY THOUGHT HE LACKED CURIOSITY, AND FOR THIS REASON HE WAS SOMEWHAT SLANDERED.** 99
>
> —THE NORSE SAGAS, DESCRIBING VIKING REACTION TO BJARNI'S JOURNEY

This is the page from the Flateyjarbok, the Norse saga that describes Bjarni's journey, as well as Eriksson's. Written in the 1300s, it is based on manuscripts and oral histories that date back centuries earlier.

CHILDREN'S CRUSADE

The tragic crusade that gave birth to a legendary story.

In 1212, a French shepherd boy named Stephen of Cloyes had a vision. The intense blue-eyed youth told everyone that Jesus had called on him to raise an army of children to win back the Holy Land. He began preaching to crowds of people. His appeal struck a chord among devout Christians ashamed of the atrocities of earlier Crusades. Perhaps the pure of heart could succeed where the corrupt armies that had gone before had failed.

Tens of thousands of children were enlisted in the Children's Crusade. Across France and Germany, village after village was emptied of its young people. Some were orphans, but many others were sent by parents who believed they were doing God's will. The children marched off in high spirits, chanting hymns, confident of victory. But they would never see Jerusalem, and only a handful ever made it back.

Thousands of German children died of hunger and exposure during an agonizing march across the Alps. Fate had even worse things in store for the

French children. More than a thousand, including Stephen, perished when their ships sank crossing the stormy Mediterranean. Several thousand survived the journey only to be sold into slavery by the merchants who had transported them.

This tragedy inspired a folktale that lives to this day, born of collective guilt and the need for someone to blame, a dark story of a town whose happy children are spirited away forever—by the Pied Piper.

> **MANY THOUGHT ALL THIS WAS HAPPENING NOT BECAUSE OF FOOLISHNESS, BUT BECAUSE GOD HAD INSPIRED THEM.**
>
> —THIRTEENTH-CENTURY GERMAN WRITER

THE CRUSADER BOYS.

Stephen believed that when his army of children reached the Mediterranean, the seas would part for them. Puzzled when that failed to happen, they were delighted when two merchants offered to ferry them across. The merchants, however— Hugh "The Iron" and William "The Pig"— betrayed the children, taking them to Egypt instead of Palestine and selling them to slave traders.

Stephen's vision inspired a twelve-year-old German boy from Cologne named Nicholas. Encouraged by his father, Nicholas recruited German children for the Crusade and led them across the Alps. When parents in Cologne eventually learned the fate of their children, they dragged Nicholas's father out of his house and hanged him.

GET OFF THE FIELD

A bevy of kings who had a real problem with sports.

In 1314, English King Edward II issued a royal edict banning the game of soccer. The sport bore little resemblance to the game played today. It often pitted town against town, with hundreds of players on a side brawling across fields or down roads. It was very popular, but nevertheless the king threatened players with harsh prison terms.

Other British kings followed suit. Edward III, Richard II, and Henry IV issued their own bans. In 1457, King James II of Scotland banned soccer *and* golf. In 1491, Scottish King James IV issued this decree:

"It is statute and ordained that in no place of the Realme there be used Fute-ball, Golf, or uther unprofitable sports."

So what was it about soccer and golf and "uther" sports that was so upsetting? The kings considered them "unprofitable" because they were distracting men from archery practice, which was essential to the defense of their countries. Without a populace of trained archers, they couldn't raise effective armies in times of crisis.

But kings' edicts ultimately proved no match for men's passion for sport. The laws were ignored and eventually forgotten. Soccer and golf continued to thrive, despite the kings who considered them to be a royal pain.

> **WE COMMAND AND FORBID ON BEHALF OF THE KING, ON PAIN OF IMPRISONMENT, SUCH GAME TO BE USED.**
>
> —EDWARD II, BANNING SOCCER IN 1314

ARCHER AND CROSS BOWMAN.

Not all royalty was down on golf. Mary Queen of Scots was an avid golfer. She paid the price for it in 1563, when she was castigated for taking to the links shortly after the murder of her husband (in which she may have had a hand).

IBN BATTUTA

Journey across the globe with the greatest traveler you never heard of.

We've all heard of the amazing travels of Marco Polo. But Ibn Battuta, who began a lifetime of wandering the year after Polo's death, traveled even farther. From his home in Morocco he set out, in 1325, on a one-year pilgrimage to Mecca that turned into a thirty-year adventure and made him the foremost frequent traveler of medieval times.

After crossing the Sahara to visit Mecca, he toured Iraq and Persia. Then he embarked on a sea journey down the coast of Africa as far as modern Tanzania. Deciding to travel by land to India and seek employment with a sultan, he took a detour to visit Constantinople in the company of a Turkish princess.

Reaching India, he settled down for eight years, working as a judge for the sultan of Delhi. The sultan then made him an envoy to China, but his mission ended in a disastrous shipwreck off the coast of India. After visiting Sri Lanka and the Maldive Islands, he finally found his way to China before beginning the long journey home.

Upon his return to Morocco, the itch to travel led Battuta on two more voyages: one northward to modern-day Spain, the other south to Mali.

Traveling by foot and camel and ship, in an age when even a hundred miles seemed a vast distance, Battuta logged an astonishing seventy-three thousand miles, visiting what today are forty-four different countries.

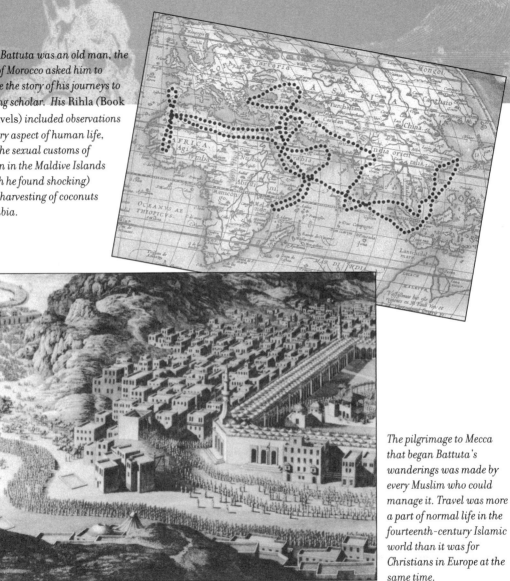

When Battuta was an old man, the ruler of Morocco asked him to dictate the story of his journeys to a young scholar. His Rihla (Book of Travels) included observations on every aspect of human life, from the sexual customs of women in the Maldive Islands (which he found shocking) to the harvesting of coconuts in Arabia.

The pilgrimage to Mecca that began Battuta's wanderings was made by every Muslim who could manage it. Travel was more a part of normal life in the fourteenth-century Islamic world than it was for Christians in Europe at the same time.

ADMIRAL ZHENG'S VOYAGES

The little-known Chinese explorer who makes Columbus look small-time.

The Age of Discovery conjures up images of intrepid Europeans seeking passage to the mysterious East. But starting in 1405, Chinese Admiral Zheng He led a series of spectacular voyages—to the West.

Zheng commanded a fleet of 300 vessels, some nearly five times the size of Columbus's ships. His ships were served by 28 thousand men (as compared with the 90 men on the *Niña*, the *Pinta*, and the *Santa Maria*). Over the course of seven voyages, Zheng's fleet journeyed as far as the southern tip of Africa—not in search of treasure or trade, but to show off the might and power of the Ming Dynasty. Recent research holds out the tantalizing possibility he may have gone even farther, sailing a huge fleet around the Cape of Good Hope and piloting it as far as Europe or even across the Atlantic to the Caribbean—all more than seventy-five years before the voyages of Columbus.

Just as remarkable as the boldness of these exploits is the speed with which they came to an end. In 1433, shortly after Zheng's last voyage, Confucian scholars convinced the emperor that such expeditions were too costly, that China should turn its focus inward and isolate itself from the rest of the world. By 1500, the Chinese court had made it a capital offense to build an oceangoing ship, and struck Admiral Zheng's accomplishments from the official record.

As Europe was broadening its horizons and sending explorers out across the globe, China was closing its doors.

Admiral Zheng often returned from his journeys with exotic animals for the emperor's zoo. The first giraffe came to Beijing in September of 1414. The Chinese were convinced it was a legendary animal from their folklore, the chi-lin, and it was believed to be an omen that the heavens favored them.

Admiral Zheng's biggest ship was the treasure ship. Measuring 440 feet long and 180 feet in beam, it was powered by nine masts carrying billowing red silk sales. The ship was loaded with gold, silver, oils, and silks, which the Chinese gave as gifts to other countries to show off their own wealth and power.

COUNT VLAD

The murderous prince who will live in legend forever.

In the 1450s there lived a prince known as Vlad the Impaler. He was ruler of Walachia, a small principality in what is now Romania. Much of what we know about Vlad comes from his enemies, and it paints a rather dark picture. He ruled with an iron hand and had no mercy for those who disobeyed him. He impaled people by the thousands, and sometimes washed down his meals with their blood.

Stories of his cruelty abound. He is said to have skinned unfaithful lovers alive. When two visiting ambassadors refused to remove their hats, saying it was not the custom in their country, Vlad replied with grim humor that he would like to support their customs—and he ordered the hats nailed to their heads. A charming fellow, Prince Vlad.

After his death, in 1476, people tried hard to forget him—but the scary stories of his short time in power never really went away. In the 1890s Vlad achieved a special sort of immortality when a writer doing research at the British Museum came across an old manuscript about him. Its tale of un-varnished evil inspired Bram Stoker to create one of the darkest characters of all time.

Vlad's father was known as Dracul, which in Romanian means "Dragon" or "Devil." Vlad was the son of the Devil.

Dracula.

In 1459, an invading Turkish army came across a gruesome warning left by Vlad: the decaying bodies of perhaps twenty thousand Turkish captives, impaled on stakes. But Vlad also impaled his own subjects as punishment for almost any crime. One estimate says he may have personally authorized the killing of as many as a hundred thousand of the half million people in his principality.

> **THE SHOCKING STORY OF A MONSTER AND BERSERKER CALLED DRACULA.**
>
> —TITLE PAGE FROM A FIFTEENTH-CENTURY ACCOUNT OF COUNT VLAD

Although he was prince of Walachia, Vlad was actually born, appropriately enough, in nearby Transylvania. He spent more time as a prisoner of other rulers than he did on the throne. His longest stretch of rule lasted only six years. He was eventually killed in battle, trying, unsuccessfully, to retake his land from the Turks.

ROUND, NOT FLAT

Did people in 1492 really think Columbus would fall off the edge of the earth?

I If you thought Columbus had to convince people the world was round—you've been had, by a writer named Washington Irving. Irving is well known today for short stories like "Rip Van Winkle" and "The Legend of Sleepy Hollow." But in 1828 he wrote a best-selling history book about Columbus. One chapter described a dramatic confrontation in which Columbus sought to win over a gathering of disbelieving Spanish scholars who argued that the world was flat.

Nice story. The truth is that Aristotle proved the earth was round two thousand years earlier, pointing out the curved shadow it casts on the moon. By Columbus's time, virtually all learned people took that for granted.

Columbus really did meet with the scholars, but the argument he had with them was about something completely different: the *size* of the globe. And Columbus was flat out wrong: he thought the earth was small enough that it would be a short sail to India.

But Irving's romanticized version made Columbus the enlightened hero overcoming myth and superstition. That's what people wanted to believe, and that's what became enshrined as history.

Irving was already one of America's best-known writers when he wrote the book on Columbus. In light of his fame, many state legislatures enthusiastically made the book required reading for schoolchildren, thus assuring that Irving's version of events would long endure in the national consciousness.

" **A SIMPLE MARINER . . . MAINTAINING HIS THEORY WITH NATURAL ELOQUENCE.** "

—WASHINGTON IRVING, *THE LIFE AND VOYAGES OF CHRISTOPHER COLUMBUS*

What set Christopher Columbus apart was not his belief that the world was round, but his persistence. He spent nearly a decade pestering Ferdinand and Isabella of Spain before he finally was able to get funding that allowed him to set forth on what he called "the enterprise of the Indies."

END OF AN EMPIRE

Discover one of the most extraordinary feats in military history.

I n 1533, a highly advanced civilization lay spread across the Andes Mountains. The Incas commanded an empire that stretched three thousand miles and was about twice the size of Texas. It boasted paved roads, intricate fortifications as good as any in the world, and an army of eighty thousand men. Over the centuries this empire had also accumulated a vast supply of gold.

That's what attracted Spanish conquistador Francisco Pizarro. After arriving on the scene, however, his band of soldiers became terrified by the numbers and might of the Incas, and feared for their lives. Still, their thirst for riches knew no bounds, and they were willing to risk everything to get their hands on all that gold.

So Pizzaro conceived a plan that was breathtaking both in its daring and in its ruthlessness. He and his men tricked the all-powerful emperor of the Incas, Atahualpa, into attending a meeting with them. Then they staged a bloody ambush, killing thousands of Atahualpa's men so they could capture the emperor himself. It proved to be a masterstroke that threw the Incas into

disarray, and eventually enabled the Spaniards to subjugate the entire empire. The cities and fortifications of this once proud people were reduced to ruins.

The most amazing thing is that Pizarro even had the nerve to undertake this conquest, never mind succeed at it. True, the Spaniards had superior weapons—crossbows and guns—but only enough for a handful of their soldiers. It remains an astonishing fact that he toppled a well-defended empire of 6 million warlike people—with just 150 men.

Pizzaro was a perfect example of the expression "He who lives by the sword dies by the sword." After a lifetime of treachery and violence, even toward his own country-men, he was surprised and killed by a band of assassins as he ate dinner in the governor's palace in Peru. The assassins were there to avenge the death of a fellow conquistador whom Pizzaro had first cheated, then executed.

Desperate to negotiate his release, Atahualpa offered the Spaniards a stupendous ransom: a room full of gold in return for his freedom. They took the gold, and then took his life. They were ready to burn him at the stake until he made a last-minute conversion to Christian-ity. Then they showed a unique brand of mercy. They hanged him instead.

DISAPPEARING DAYS

*Ten days lost from
the calendar forever.*

What if you went to sleep and woke up ten days later? It happened to millions of people in Europe in October of 1582, and some of them were quite upset about it.

It all had to do with problems in the calendar instituted 1,628 years before by Julius Caesar. That was just the tiniest bit off, and so the world lost eleven minutes per year, for sixteen hundred years. The spring equinox had drifted from March to winter. Things were a mess.

Pope Gregory XIII took matters in hand. He appointed a committee of calendar experts to examine the problem, and they suggested a more scientifically correct model. The pope accepted their recommendations and issued a papal bull mandating the changes.

But to get things back on schedule, ten days had to be slashed. So on October 4, 1582, much of western Europe went to sleep and woke up the next morning on October 15. Reaction was mixed. The citizens of Frankfurt, Germany, rioted against the pope, who they thought was trying to steal days from their lives. On the other hand, peasants living in isolated rural villages barely noticed at all.

Some countries didn't accept the change for years, creating massive confusion. But eventually everyone let go of the missing days and adopted the Gregorian Calendar we still use today.

Pope Gregory was eighty years old when he fixed his signature on the papal bull making changes to Caesar's calendar. Those changes proved remarkably accurate: the Gregorian Calendar is off by only one day every three thousand years.

Protestant England rejected the new calendar and didn't adopt it for over for 170 years. When it finally did so, protesters took to the streets shouting, "Give us back our eleven days," or chanting this antireform, anti-Catholic ditty:

In seventeen hundred and
fifty-three
The style it was changed
to popery.

UP WITH *UPPOWOC*

From the American colonies: an herbal cure that ignited world interest.

In 1585, Sir Walter Raleigh organized a British expedition to establish a new colony in Virginia. He sent along twenty-five-year-old Thomas Hariot as a historian and surveyor. Hariot spent a year at the Roanoke Colony and wrote a report detailing his experiences—the first book in English about the New World.

In his account, Hariot told of discovering an astonishing herbal remedy, called *uppowoc*, cultivated by the local tribes. It "openeth all the pores and passages," Hariot marveled, "whereby their bodies are notably preserved in health and know not many grievous diseases, wherewithal we in England are often times afflicted." Intrigued, the colonists tried this herbal concoction themselves, and had so many "rare and wonderful" experiences with it that they brought a load back to introduce to England.

Uppowoc created a lasting sensation upon reaching the shores of Britain. It is still with us, but now we take a different view of its medicinal qualities. We also call it by a different name, its Spanish name.

Tobacco.

One of the first antismoking fanatics was King James I of England. He called smoking "a custom loathsome to the eye, hateful to the nose, harmful to the brain, dangerous to the lungs." In 1605 he increased tobacco taxes 4,000 percent in a failed attempt to stop people from smoking.

In his book, which enjoyed much popularity in England, Hariot claimed that uppowoc was so esteemed by the Indians that sometimes they would throw it upon the fire as a sacrifice to the gods.

COFFEE AND THE POPE

When you drink your morning coffee tomorrow, say thanks to the pope who made it all possible.

A coffee craze first gripped the world about six hundred years ago in the Middle East. Some of the earliest coffee fanatics were Muslim mystics, trying to stay awake for nighttime worship. As coffee became popular, it also became controversial. Early coffeehouses were such brewing grounds for radical ideas that authorities in Mecca and Cairo tried to outlaw the drink. The prohibitions proved ineffective.

When coffee hit Europe in the late 1500s, priests at the Vatican argued that it was a satanic concoction of Islamic infidels. Accordingly, they thought it should be banned. That's when Pope Clement VIII stepped in. After giving coffee a taste, he gave his blessing to the bean.

"This Satan's drink is so delicious," he supposedly said, "it would be a pity to let the infidels have exclusive use of it. We shall fool Satan by baptizing it."

With this papal blessing, coffee soon began to conquer Europe, and become the morning necessity it remains for many people today.

Clement VIII may have given coffee his blessing, but that doesn't mean everyone fell instantly in love with it. In 1610, British poet Sir George Sandys described the bitter brew this way: "Black as soote, and tasting not much unlike it."

66 **THIS IS THE BEVERAGE OF THE FRIENDS OF GOD.** 99

—"IN PRAISE OF COFFEE," ARABIC POEM, 1511

With a Starbucks on every corner, you might think coffee has never been more popular, but that's nothing compared to the popularity it enjoyed in the Middle East during the 1500s. In Turkey, a woman could divorce a man who did not provide her with enough coffee.

ONE SWEET DEAL

*A spicy swap
unlike anything
else in history.*

In the early 1600s, Great Britain and Holland were vying for control over the valuable Spice Islands in the East Indies. All but forgotten today, these tiny islands were at one time considered prize possessions because of the nutmeg and cloves that could be found there and nowhere else. The British and the Dutch spent years battling for control of the lucrative trade.

In 1616, British captain Nathaniel Courthope staked a claim on the island of Run, which contained one of the world's only known nutmeg forests. With only a ragtag band of sailors and natives, Courthope fended off Dutch attacks for nearly four years. But there was a spy among his men who eventually betrayed him to the Dutch. They murdered Courthope and finally took the island in 1620.

The British, however, steadfastly maintained that Run was rightfully theirs. And they continued to wage war with the Dutch. Years later, when the two nations were ready to sign a peace treaty, the island was still a bone of contention. So to sweeten the deal, the Dutch offered to hand over the rights to another remote island in return.

The island's name: Manhattan.

A forest of nutmeg for the Big Apple—not a bad deal.

Nutmeg was especially valued as a spice, not simply because of its taste but also because it was believed to cure the plague. Once the Dutch gained control of the world's nutmeg supply, they plotted to keep prices high and to prevent nutmeg plants from falling into British hands.

This is a map of Manhattan from 1638, when it was still a Dutch possession, inhabited by just a handful of people. Staten Island, already bearing that name, can be seen in the upper left.

BEER AND THE *MAYFLOWER*

How a thirst for beer played a role in the colonizing of America.

The *Mayflower* was headed for Virginia when storms blew it off course. It ended up hitting the shore of Massachusetts. Rather than heading south to find a better location for their colony, the Pilgrims put ashore at Plymouth Rock.

One Pilgrim's journal explains why: "We could not take time for further search or consideration, our victuals being much spent, especially our beere."

Yes, the Pilgrims made port because they ran out of beer. In those days beer was considered an essential and healthy part of everyone's daily diet—water, on the other hand, was usually considered suspect, because it easily became contaminated with disease. The *Mayflower* had set out from England loaded with beer barrels that were now running out.

Once ashore, the Pilgrims promptly erected a brew house and got to work brewing up a new batch to slake their thirst. So Plymouth, Massachusetts, became the historic home of the Pilgrims … because they needed to make a beer run.

WELCOME, ENGLISHMAN. I AM SAMOSET. DO YOU HAVE ANY BEER?

—THE FIRST WORDS OF THE INDIAN SAMOSET WHEN HE ASTONISHED THE PILGRIMS BY WALKING INTO THEIR COLONY AND GREETING THEM IN ENGLISH IN MARCH OF 1621. HE HAD LEARNED THE LANGUAGE FROM HIS CONTACT WITH ENGLISH FISHING VESSELS.

One of the Pilgrims who came ashore that day was a young man there strictly for the beer—in a manner of speaking. John Alden was hired for the journey as a cooper, primarily to make beer barrels. British law required that "whosever shall carry Beer beyond the sea" had to bring a cooper along to make replacement barrels, since barrels back in England were always in short supply. Otherwise John never would have had a chance to romance Priscilla.

SHAKESPEARE IN PRINT

A world without Macbeth, Hamlet, or Romeo? It almost happened.

Shakespeare's genius was never fully appreciated during his lifetime. People thought of him as just another playwright. Since he never published his plays, the only ones in print were pirated versions often missing whole scenes. Once he was dead and buried, much of his work was forgotten. And it might have remained so but for two loyal friends.

After the Bard of Avon passed on, actors John Heminge and Henry Condell took it upon themselves, in their words, "to keep the memory of so worthy a Friend & Fellow alive, as was our Shakespeare." They determined to publish a collection of all his dramatic works. It was a task that took them years to accomplish.

The two men had acted alongside Shakespeare in his plays, and they knew his work in detail. They searched out long-lost copies, dredged up missing pages, and convinced playwright Ben Jonson to help them edit the material. They scratched together funds for the project, and finally, seven years after Shakespeare's death, they were able to publish the plays in one authoritative volume, now known as the First Folio.

"To be or not to be?" Much of Shakespeare wouldn't be, if not for two devoted fans.

Mr. WILLIAM
SHAKESPEARES
COMEDIES,
HISTORIES, &
TRAGEDIES.

Published according to the True Originall Copies.

LONDON
Printed by Isaac Iaggard, and Ed. Blount. 1623.

*From the most able, to him that can but spell:
here you are number'd."* So begins the note to "the
reat Variety of Readers" that opens the First Folio.
Heminge and Condell were obviously confident
hat the book would have mass appeal, and they
ontinued in a manner both witty and brazenly
nercantile: *"Well! It is now publique, & you wil
tand for your priuiledges wee know: to read, and
ensure. Do so, but buy it first."*

*Heminge and Condell
acted in many of Shake-
speare's plays at the
Globe Theatre, and were
probably among his
closest friends. But
their main occupation
seems to have been
fathering children—
they had twenty-one
between them.*

TULIPOMANIA

A fast-growing investment that was quick to wilt.

I n the fall of 1636, it wasn't the Dow or the Nasdaq that investors in the Netherlands were watching, but the price of the tulip. The flower had become a passion in this nation of gardeners, with demand far outstripping supply.

The Netherlands had recently come out of a depression and its citizens had money to burn. The buying and selling of bulbs turned to a frenzied speculation on bulb futures. As prices shot up—sometimes doubling in a week—bricklayers, tradesmen, clergymen, and lawyers all became day traders trying to cash in on the market.

Prices quickly rose to irrational levels. Toward the end of the craze, some of the rarest tulip bulbs were being sold at a price equivalent to $100,000 today.

Then, in February of 1637, the bottom suddenly dropped out of the market. Dealers panicked and the price of bulbs fell to 1 percent of their previous value—sometimes less. Paper profits were wiped out, and tulipomania was over almost as quickly as it began.

The most prized varieties of tulips were ones that were almost entirely yellow or white, with brilliant streaks of violet or red. It is a delicious irony to note that these tulips were in fact diseased, infected by a virus unique to tulips.

A price of 3,000 guilders was not un-common for a prized bulb. A writer in 1637 pointed out that this extraordinary sum could also purchase all of the following:

8 pigs	4 barrels of beer
4 oxen	2 tons of butter
12 sheep	1,000 pounds of
24 tons of wheat	cheese
48 tons of rye	1 silver cup
2 hogshead of wine	new clothes
1 ship	1 bed

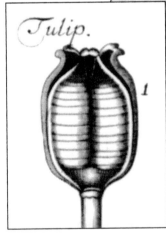

Tulip.

1

FIT FOR A KING

An opulent palace inspired by a fit of royal envy?

I t was a party to end all parties, all the guests agreed, held in honor of the young French King Louis XIV. Host Nicholas Fouquet, France's Minister of Finance, had in essence invited the boss home for dinner, and taken great pains to impress him. The food was delicious, the music sublime, the entertainment fantastic; the great writer Molière wrote a light comedy especially for the occasion.

Most amazing of all, perhaps, was the site of the party. It took place on Fouquet's luxurious estate, Vaux-le-Vicomte. Fouquet had spared no expense in building a home with no equal, combining spectacular architecture and breathtaking gardens. He was able to entertain King Louis on a scale that the king himself might have a hard time matching.

Big mistake.

Louis was impressed, even envious, but not pleased in the least. The royal scale of the surroundings helped convince him that the rumors he heard were true: Fouquet must be skimming public funds, perhaps with an eye to setting himself up as ruler of France. Louis ordered Fouquet arrested and jailed. The evidence was inconclusive, so Fouquet avoided a death sentence, but he was never to know freedom again.

The Sun King exacted a sweet revenge against Fouquet for arousing his jealousy and suspicion. He hired the jailed man's architect, designer, and landscaper to build him an even grander palace, so he would never have to be jealous again.

A palace called Versailles.

Protesting his innocence,
Fouquet was exiled to a
fortress in Italy, where he
spent the last two decades
of his life in what amounted
to solitary confinement. It
was a far cry from the life
he imagined here at Vaux-
le-Vicomte, with its lovely
grounds dotted by 250
fountains.

Louis XIV did not take kindly to anyone who he felt
was treading on royal prerogatives. His political
philosophy was summed up in a memorable saying:
"L'état c'est moi!"—I am the state.

THE SIEGE THAT GAVE BIRTH TO THE CROISSANT

An invading Turkish army provides the inspiration for a breakfast delicacy.

The croissant is not French—it was first baked in Austria. And its shape is anything but an accident. The popular pastry dates back to 1683. In that year an army of more than a hundred thousand Ottoman Turks was besieging the city of Vienna. They surrounded it for months, and residents inside the stout walls began to wonder if each day would be their last.

When the Turks tried tunneling under the walls, bakers working through the night heard the digging sounds and raised the alarm. This early warning prevented the Turks from breaching Vienna's walls and helped save the city. Eventually an army under Polish King John III reached Vienna and drove the Turks away.

The bakers celebrated the end of the siege in a remarkable way. They copied the crescent moon from their enemy's flag and turned it into a commemorative pastry. It was called a *Kipfel* (German for "crescent") and it honored a victory that might never have happened but for the bakers themselves.

Kipfels turned into croissants in 1770, when fifteen-
year-old Austrian Princess Marie Antoinette arrived
in France to marry the future King Louis XVI.
Parisian bakers started turning out Kipfels in her
honor, and the French found themselves in love with
a breakfast treat that they soon made their own.

The siege of Vienna is also believed
by some to be the birthplace of the
bagel. King John of Poland was
widely known as a skilled horse-
man, and a baker supposedly
created a roll in the shape of a
stirrup to honor him. The Austrian
word for "stirrup" is bügel—
eventually Americanized to "bagel."
Can it be true that one battle did so
much for so many breakfasts?

1687

LLOYD'S OF LONDON

Sit down for a cup of Joe with your insurance agent, and you're back to where it all began.

In 1687, a new coffeehouse opened near London's riverfront. It soon became a popular spot for seafarers and traders—open around the clock and always crowded. One corner was reserved exclusively for ships' captains. For the benefit of his customers, proprietor Edward Lloyd kept a chalkboard listing the arrival and departure dates of cargo ships, along with other useful information.

Patrons found Lloyd's dimly lit booths a convenient place to negotiate insurance for future voyages. That started a trend that is still going strong more than three hundred years later. The brokers and underwriters who frequented Lloyd's eventually bought the coffeehouse and turned it into a world-class insurance association. Today, Lloyd's of London is renowned for insuring the uninsurable: a film star's legs, the "unsinkable" *Titanic*, a satellite in space.

Though he never sold any, Edward Lloyd's name is synonymous with insurance, since it all began over a cup of his coffee.

Lloyd's underwriters became famous for insuring film star Betty Grable's legs for $1 million. More recently, Jennifer Lopez has denied reports that she asked Lloyd's to insure her derriere for $1 billion. A food critic insured his taste buds at Lloyd's, male strippers have sought policies protecting their crown jewels, and a comedy troupe once covered themselves against the possibility that someone in the audience might actually die laughing.

Lloyd's has run into some tough times lately. It lost more than $3 billion in claims stemming from the attack on the World Trade Center—its biggest loss ever from a single event.

Lloyd's might never have opened if King Charles II had had his way. About ten years earlier, in 1676, the king had issued a "Proclamation for the Suppression of Coffee Houses." Hundreds of them dotted London, and the king called them "the great resort of the idle and disaffected." The outcry of coffee drinkers was so great that just ten days later he backed down and withdrew the proclamation. A few decades later, though, coffee began to lose ground in Britain to an even more popular beverage: tea, imported from China.

PAPER TRAIL

A walk in the woods that changed everything.

Beginning in the 1600s, Europe was hit with a crippling shortage. People had to deal with the fact that a valuable commodity was in increasingly short supply. What was it?

Rags.

Rags were used to make paper, and paper was in great demand. Publishers of books, newspapers, and political pamphlets all clamored for more paper. But there just weren't enough rags. Advertisements appeared asking women to save their rags. In 1666, England banned the use of cotton and linen for the burial of the dead, decreeing they must be saved for making paper. One entrepreneur even suggested using the cloth from Egyptian mummies. The scarcity of rags lead to fearful paper shortages in Europe and America.

Then a French scientist took a walk in the woods.

René-Antoine Ferchault de Réaumur was an accomplished physicist and chemist. He was also a man who loved bugs. Walking in the woods one day, he came upon an abandoned wasps' nest. Delighted, he began to examine it in detail, and an astounding fact dawned on him: the nest was made of paper, paper made by wasps, paper made *without* the use of rags. How?

By chewing wood and plant fibers.

What wasps could do, he argued, man could find a way to do also. It took decades, but his discovery was the spark that inspired inventors to discover methods for making paper from wood pulp. Thanks to Réaumur's nature walk, we can now do what would have once been considered almost criminal: crumple up a piece of paper and throw it out.

The invention of rag paper is credited to a Chinese eunuch named Ts'ai Lun in the year 105. Until then the Chinese were writing on pieces of bamboo, which was awkward, or on scrolls of silk, which were very expensive.

Paper is so plentiful today that the average office worker uses ten thousand sheets a year—and thinks nothing of it. Of course, the flip side of that is deforestation—every year an area of tropical rain forest the size of North Carolina is cut down, in part to meet the world's paper needs.

Americans !
Encourage your own Manufactories, and they will Improve.

LADIES. fave your RAGS.

AS the Subfcribers have it in contemplation to erect a PA-PER-MILL in *Dalton*, the enfuing fpring; and the bufinefs being very ben-eficial to the community at large, they flatter themfelves that they fhall meet with due encouragement. And that every wo-man, who has the good of her country, and the intereft of her own family at heart, will patronize them, by faving her rags, and fending them to their Manu-factory, or to the nearest S...
for which the S...

ENGLISH KILT

Horrors! Can it be true that the Scottish kilt was invented by an Englishman?

I n the 1700s, the traditional dress of Scottish highlanders was the *plaide* (pronounced *play-dee*), a large blanket wrapped around the body, thrown over the shoulder, and belted at the waist.

It was cheap, convenient, and great for cold nights hanging out in the heath—but it could be awfully cumbersome for industrial workers. At least that's how Englishman Tom Rawlinson saw it. Rawlinson came to Scotland in 1727 to open an iron foundry. He employed a "throng of Highlanders," but found their *plaides* often got in their way. He summoned a tailor to help him make the traditional dress a bit more practical. The tailor responded by shearing the *plaide* in two, cutting the skirt into a separate garment.

So was born what we now know as the kilt.

After a Scottish uprising in 1745, it was banned by the British government. That had just the impact you might expect—it made the kilt infinitely more popular with Scots hostile to British rule, even though this most traditional of Scottish garments owes its existence to an Englishman.

When the British government banned the kilt in 1746, it exempted the Highland regiments in the British army. During the thirty-five years the ban stayed in force, Scots serving in the British army were the only ones who could legally wear kilts.

It's bad enough that the kilt originated with an Englishman, but to make things even worse, bagpipes aren't Scottish either. The earliest known references to bagpipes date back to ancient Greece, and the instrument probably originated in the Middle East. Here a Jordanian honor guard plays the pipes.

FROM SIN TO GRACE

The story of a slave trader who left us an amazing legacy.

John Newton started in the slave trade at age twenty. He eventually became captain of his own slave ship. "I was once an active instrument in a business at which my heart now shudders," he later wrote.

On May 10, 1748, his ship was floundering in a storm. Until then, Newton had never been a religious man, but as the storm threatened to capsize the ship, he fell to his knees and began to pray. "God have mercy," he begged as wave after wave crashed violently over the deck. When the storm suddenly died down, he vowed to devote himself to God.

That moment changed his life forever, and one day it would touch the lives of millions.

It took years, but driven by his new faith, Newton left the slave trade and became a minister. Eventually he started to speak out against slavery, and turned into a crusading supporter of abolition.

He also became well known for writing hymns. One song that we remember particularly well today celebrated his own *amazing* transformation.

Amazing Grace, how sweet the sound,
That saved a wretch like me.
I once was lost, but now am found,
Was blind, but now I see.

Newton was at first rejected for ordination to the ministry because of his check-ered past. He was eventually allowed to become a minister in 1764, and continued in the ministry for forty-three years. He lived long enough to see the slave trade abolished by the British Empire in 1807... in part because of his efforts.

" I AWAITED WITH FEAR AND IMPATIENCE TO RECEIVE MY INEVITABLE DOOM. "

—JOHN NEWTON,
DESCRIBING THE STORM

TO BE SOLD, on board the Ship *Bance-Island*, on tuefday the 6th of *May* next, at *Afhley-Ferry*; a choice cargo of about 250 fine healthy

NEGROES,

juft arrived from the Windward & Rice Coaft. —The utmoft care has already been taken, and fhall be continued, to keep them free from the leaft danger of being infected with the SMALL-POX, no boat having been on board, and all other communication with people from *Charles-Town* prevented.
Auftin, Laurens, & Appleby.

Newton continued in the slave trade for five years after his conversion, finding it disagreeable but not yet considering it morally wrong. "What I did, I did ignorantly," he said later.

MOVE OVER, PAUL REVERE

Listen, my children, and you shall hear of a rider even greater than Paul Revere.

Everyone's heard of Paul Revere. His midnight ride on the eighteenth of April in 1775 to warn of British troops marching toward Lexington and Concord has become a part of American folklore. But another epic ride, which began the following day, has been largely forgotten.

Hours after hearing that British troops had opened fire on colonial farmers in what became known as the Battle of Lexington, the Massachusetts Provincial Congress issued a call to arms, asking neighboring colonies for help. Israel Bissell, a twenty-three-year-old dispatch rider, was sent south to spread the news of the Revolution.

Under his spurs, his horse seemed to take wing. Local legend has it that he made Worcester, a day's ride, in just two hours, and that his horse dropped dead when he got there. With a new horse, Bissell was off again. Through Connecticut he raced, then to New York, and on to Philadelphia. Astonishingly, he rode 350 miles in just six days, a record time.

Paul Revere, by contrast, rode only twenty miles. But Revere's effort to "spread the alarm to every Middlesex village and farm" were immortalized by Henry Wadsworth Longfellow. Nobody wrote a poem about Israel Bissell, so he wound up one of history's has-beens.

In 1995, Massachusetts poet Clay Perry finally gave Bissell a poem of his own. It begins:

Listen my children, to my epistle:
Of the long, long ride of Israel Bissell;
Who outrode Paul by miles and time;
But didn't rate a poet's rhyme.

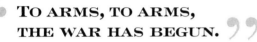

" TO ARMS, TO ARMS, THE WAR HAS BEGUN. "

—DISPATCH RIDER ISRAEL BISSELL

This is the message Bissell carried. Addressed to "all Friends of American Liberty," it detailed the encounter in Lexington and charged Bissell to "alarm the Country" with the news. It resides now at the Pennsylvania Historical Society.

THE COLONEL AND THE NOTE

How did procrastination change the outcome of the American Revolution?

On a freezing cold Christmas night, George Washington brought the tattered remnants of his army across the Delaware. His troops were in wretched shape, decimated by previous battles, worn out, ill fed. Nonetheless, Washington was leading them on a surprise attack on Hessian soldiers occupying Trenton, New Jersey.

The Hessian commander, Colonel Johann Rall, was attending a Christmas party that night. To him it was inconceivable that the disorganized colonials would dare to mount an attack. Around midnight a local farmer, a British sympathizer, came to the door with a message. A servant took the message and gave it to Rall, but the colonel didn't want to interrupt his card game. He stuffed the note in his pocket—unread.

At daybreak, in a freezing sleet, Washington and his sleep-starved troops attacked. Their powder was so wet that many of them couldn't fire their weapons, so they charged with bayonets or used their muskets as clubs. The groggy Hessians received quite a Christmas surprise—in fact, they were completely overwhelmed. Nine hundred Hessians were taken prisoner and Colonel Rall was mortally wounded. As a doctor cut away his clothes to treat his wounds, the note fell from his pocket.

It turned out to be a message warning of Washington's approach. If he'd taken the time to read it earlier, Rall might have lived to see the Americans defeated, and Washington his prisoner.

Before he died, Colonel Rall had a chance to look at the message that could have turned the tables. "If I had read this," he said mournfully, "I would not be here."

Washington and Greene Visiting the Dying Rall After the Battle of Trenton

66 **THOSE CLOD-HOPPERS WILL NOT ATTACK US!** 99

—COLONEL RALL THE DAY
BEFORE THE BATTLE

Preparing to cross the Delaware, Washington stepped into a boat containing Colonel Henry Knox. He gave the three-hundred-pound officer a nudge with his toe, and uttered these immortal words, which gave a much-needed lift to his cold and miserable troops: "Shift that fat ass, Harry. But slowly, or you'll swamp the damn boat!"

FIRST PRESIDENT

Discover the amazing truth about our nation's first president.

George Washington is revered as the Father of Our Country. He was not, however, our first president. Washington was the first president elected under the Constitution, taking office in 1789. But the United States came together as a nation years before the Constitution was enacted. In 1781, when the last of the thirteen colonies ratified the Articles of Confederation, the new country was officially brought into being.

Shortly thereafter, Congress unanimously elected John Hanson of Maryland as the first president of the United States. His full title was actually "president of the United States in Congress assembled." Congress voted to provide the new president with a house and servants, and ruled that he "takes precedence of all and every person in the United States."

Hanson served only a year and is now largely forgotten, but at the time, a colleague wrote: "I congratulate your Excellency on your appointment to fill the most important seat in the United States."

That letter was signed by none other than George Washington.

Under Hanson's leadership, Congress established the Treasury Department, adopted the Great Seal of the United States (still in use today), and declared the fourth Thursday of every November "a day of Thanksgiving."

The Articles of Confederation were, in a sense, the first constitution. They became the law of the land on March 1, 1781, a date that could be considered the country's birthday. They were in effect for nearly eight years, a period of time often forgotten in American history.

General George Washington referred to Hanson as "the president" in his correspondence. If Hanson was the first president, what would that make Washington? After Hanson, there were six more presidents elected by Congress, one each session, before the Constitution was ratified. So Washington would be the country's eighth president.

DOCTOR OF DEATH

A medical man's humane gesture turns into a symbol of terror.

After the outbreak of the French Revolution, a doctor and member of the National Assembly beseeched his fellow revolutionaries to outlaw inhumane forms of execution.

He described in detail gory executions of the past, and advocated a less painful method. He painted a vivid picture of what he had in mind: "The mechanism falls like lighting; the head flies off; the blood spurts; the man no longer exists."

Dr. Joseph Guillotin became an instant celebrity after championing this new means of execution, and although he neither invented nor designed the device that was subsequently built, his name was quickly attached to it. The guillotine soon took center stage in the Revolution, as fourteen thousand "enemies of the state" were brought before huge crowds to lie beneath its blade—including King Louis XVI and his queen, Marie Antoinette.

After the doctor's death, in 1814, his children changed their names—appalled that their once-proud family moniker was now synonymous with bloody decapitation and revolutionary terror.

Before the guillotine was adopted, Paris executioner Charles-Henri Sanson wrote a memo complaining that death by decapitation was becoming, well, a bit of a headache. Each beheading blunted his blade, he owned only two swords, and there were just too many people to be executed. The result, he said, was that many executions were unavoidably cruel.

Many condemned prisoners carefully rehearsed their walk to the guillotine while in prison, so they could put on a gallant show before the crowd at the hour of their death. One man said to the executioner: "Today's the actual performance; you'll be surprised at how well I know my role."

THE MECHANICAL INTERNET

How networking came to Europe more than two hundred years ago.

I n the 1790s, dozens of odd-looking towers sprouted up across France. They comprised the backbone of a new, state-of-the-art communications network.

The towers were the brainchild of a French inventor named Claude Chappe. Each one had mechanical arms that could be rotated into ninety different positions, visible ten miles away. An operator would set the arms in a certain position, then the operator in the next tower would see that through a telescope and set his arms in the same position. Messages rippled down the line at more than one hundred miles an hour, astonishing for this day and age.

Chappe wanted to call his new invention the tachygraph, meaning "fast writer." But a friend convinced him to give it a different name, meaning "far writer." And so he called it…the telegraph.

When Napoleon seized power in 1799, he was quick to grasp the military advantage of high-speed communications. He ordered new lines built out from Paris in every direction. Eventually more than five hundred towers connected France's major cities. Other countries followed suit, and lines of towers snaked across Europe, Russia, and even northern Africa.

The invention of the electrical telegraph eventually made the Chappe telegraph obsolete. Today only a few of the hundreds of towers remain…silent monuments to the world's first high-speed network.

Chappe was hounded by others who claimed credit for his ideas. Eventually he became so depressed that he took his own life by throwing himself down a well.

Chappe began his experiments during the French Revolution, which caused him no end of trouble. Angry mobs twice destroyed his equipment because they suspected he was trying to communicate with jailed royalty.

WARRIOR QUEEN

The Chinese pirate whose navy became a world power.

The most successful pirate of all time was a woman. She commanded more men and ships than any other pirate in history. Best of all, from her point of view, she retired undefeated, kept all of her plunder, and was allowed to live peacefully into old age.

The name of this remarkable woman was Hsi Kai. Plucked from a Canton brothel by the notorious pirate Ching Yih, she rapidly became much more than just another concubine. Stunningly beautiful, she was also a wily negotiator and an organizational genius. In return for her hand in marriage, she demanded and got a 50 percent share of her husband's wealth. Upon his death in 1807, she took complete control of the fleet.

For three years, Hsi Kai commanded more than fifty thousand men and women and more than a thousand ships. Hers was a pirate navy larger than that of most world powers. She ruled much of the South China Sea with an iron hand, terrorizing shipping, attacking seaside villages, and defeating every naval force sent to intercept her.

By 1810, Britain, Portugal, and China were so fed up that they assembled a combined force to attack Hsi Kai. To avoid the massive loss of life such an assault would entail, the emperor of China offered amnesty: "If there is anything of a woman's heart in you, you will someday want peace and offspring. Could it be now?" She wasn't interested in children, but she knew a good deal when she saw one. Under terms she personally negotiated with the governor general of Canton, she and seventeen thousand of her men gave up their ships and weapons but were allowed to keep their stolen treasures. She lived another thirty years and died wealthy—nobody ever got the better of Hsi Kai.

Hsi Kai's fleet consisted of 200 ocean-going junks, each with 20 to 30 cannon, 800 smaller coastal vessels, and dozens of riverboats. She commanded more than fifty thousand pirates at the same time that the U.S. Navy consisted of just five thousand men. Another comparison: her fleet was nearly twice the size of the Spanish Armada.

66 **THE PIRATES ARE TOO POWERFUL, WE CANNOT MASTER THEM BY ARMS.** 99

—CHINESE ADMIRAL, 1809

si Kai laid down very strict rules for her pirates, with harsh punishment eted out to those who broke them. The rape of a female captive, for ample, was punishable by death. On the other hand, if the woman ad agreed to have sex with her captor, they were both killed—he was eheaded and she was thrown overboard.

THE REAL UNCLE SAM

How did a meat packer from Troy, New York, become the first Uncle Sam?

During the War of 1812, Sam Wilson had a contract to supply meat to U.S. troops: salted beef and pork ready to ship out in barrels. To identify the barrels, Wilson assigned a worker to letter them with the initials U.S., for "United States." That abbreviation wasn't as common as it is today, and when people asked the man doing the lettering what it meant, he joked that it really stood for Uncle Sam, the kindly meat packer's nickname.

The joke got around with amazing speed. Within months the phrase began to appear in political cartoons and newspaper editorials. People started referring to all government property as belonging to Uncle Sam. Soldiers started calling themselves "Uncle Sam's boys." In no time at all, the meat packer's nickname became the country's nickname.

In early drawings, Uncle Sam appeared clean-shaven, in black. Later he wore the colors of the flag. In the Civil War, cartoonist Thomas Nast drew him gaunt and bearded like Abe Lincoln. The most famous Uncle Sam is actually a self-portrait of artist James Montgomery Flagg.

As official artist for New York State, artist James Montgomery Flagg created more than forty-five recruiting posters during World War I. None was more famous than the one he modeled on himself. The poster was so effective it was recycled for use in World War II.

Uncle Sam and Johnny Appleseed were kin! Sam Wilson married a woman named Betsy Mann. She was a cousin of none other than John Chapman, better known as Johnny Appleseed. It's even possible that the two American icons played together as boys.

JACKSON AND BENTON

A presidential adviser with a most unusual résumé.

One of President Andrew Jackson's most trusted advisers was Missouri senator Thomas Hart Benton. Pretty extraordinary, considering that twenty years earlier, Benton and his brother had put a bullet into Jackson!

Benton was an aide to then General Jackson during the War of 1812, but the two men quarreled over an obscure point of honor. Jackson was fiercely jealous of his reputation, and had already killed one man who had insulted him. One day in Nashville he saw Benton and went after him with his pistol. It was Jackson, however, who ended up being shot twice and nearly killed.

From that moment on Benton knew that if he stayed in Tennessee, Jackson's friends would exact their revenge. "I am in the middle of hell, and see no alternative but to kill or be killed," he wrote. But he did find an alternative— he lit out for Missouri.

By the time Jackson came to Washington in the 1820s, Benton had become a powerful senator from the Show Me State. Some thought Old Hickory might shoot Benton on sight. But instead he made peace and gained an ally. Together the two men fought attempts to split the Union asunder.

Twenty years after the shooting, doctors finally removed the bullet. Jackson supposedly offered it to Benton, saying it was his property. Benton declined, saying that by carrying it for nearly twenty years, Jackson had earned the right to keep it.

Benton is considered one of the great figures in the history of the U.S. Senate, where he served for thirty years.

Violence seemed to follow Jackson around. In 1835 he became the first president to be targeted in an assassination attempt. A deranged housepainter named Richard Lawrence tried to shoot him as he walked out of the Capitol. The gun misfired, and the enraged Jackson lifted his cane to strike his attacker. Lawrence fired again with a second pistol, but when that also misfired, the sixty-seven-year-old president escaped unharmed.

THE ATTEMPTED ASSASSINATION,
OF THE PRESIDENT OF UNITED STATES JAN. 30.1835.

"THE STAR-SPANGLED BANNER"

Next time you hear our national anthem, tip your hat to the drunken redcoats who made it possible.

Washington, D.C. was aflame, thanks to British soldiers who had put it to the torch. With smoke still rising from the ruins, the Brits set out on a march through Maryland. After most of the soldiers had filed peacefully through the town of Upper Marlboro, two drunken stragglers came along shouting and carrying on. One of the town fathers, Dr. William Beanes, was so incensed with this behavior that he personally carted the drunken redcoats to jail.

But one of the men escaped and brought back more redcoats. They released the jailed soldier, seized the good doctor, and carried him off to a British frigate in Chesapeake Bay. So a lawyer friend sailed out to negotiate the doctor's release. Just as he got there, the British began shelling nearby Fort McHenry, and detained both men until the shelling was over.

And that's how a lawyer named Francis Scott Key happened to observe "bombs bursting in air." His poem "The Star-Spangled Banner" became an instant hit.

The music? Key purloined it from a tune called "To Anacreon in Heaven," which, appropriately enough, was a popular English drinking song.

The first known photo of the flag that flew over Fort McHenry was taken at the Boston Navy Yard in 1873. The thirty-two-foot-high flag was sewn by Baltimore banner maker Mary Pickersgill, whose mother had made flags for George Washington.

It took more than 40 bills and resolutions in Congress before "The Star-Spangled Banner" was finally adopted as the national anthem in 1931.

BA-BUMP GOES THE STETHOSCOPE

Who would ever think modesty could be the mother of invention?

In September of 1816, a buxom young woman paid a visit to a French physician named Dr. René Laënnec. He felt certain that she had heart problems. But the morals of the day prevented him (a bachelor) from listening to her heart in the normal fashion, by putting his ear to her chest. Besides, trying to hear a heart through such an ample bosom would be a trifle difficult.

The doctor was also a musician. He rolled a tube from paper—like a flute—and he touched this to his patient. "I was surprised and gratified," he wrote, "at being able to hear the beating of the heart with greater clearness than ever before." Soon after, he fashioned a hollow cylinder out of wood with a funnel at one end—the first stethoscope.

Many doctors were quick to adapt to this new technology. But some resisted. One American doctor put it this way: "He that hath ears to hear, let him use his ears and not a stethoscope."

But the new device allowed doctors to diagnose problems of the heart and lungs they had never been able to uncover before. A new window on illness was opened.

Thanks to modesty.

> ## THE VERY SIZE OF [THE] BREASTS WAS A PHYSICAL OBSTACLE.

—RENÉ LAËNNEC, 1819

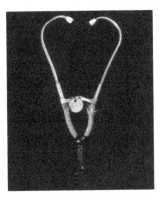

René Laënnec thought his invention was such a simple device that it didn't need a name. But when others pushed him for a name, he suggested "stethoscope"—from the Greek word stēthos, meaning "chest," and skopos, meaning "observer."

In 1852, a New York doctor named George Camman invented the modern stethoscope, with a bell-shaped chest piece and a tube running to each ear. Medicine's most ubiquitous instrument has changed very little since then.

NIGHT WRITING

The artillery captain who helped the blind to read— in spite of himself.

Imagine being a frontline soldier and getting a message at night. There's no way to read that message without lighting a lamp that will expose you to enemy fire. In the early 1800s this dilemma inspired a French artillery officer, Captain Charles Barbier, to create "night writing." It was a code consisting of raised dots poked onto a piece of paper. The code used combinations of twelve dots to stand for different sounds.

Eventually Barbier introduced his concept to the blind.

A thirteen-year-old boy at the Royal Institute for the Blind was one of the first to learn the new system. He was excited by the opportunities it offered, but thought it might be too complex, so he offered Barbier some ideas on how to simplify and improve it. The haughty Barbier did not welcome his suggestions—in fact, he was insulted that a mere boy could imagine he had something to offer. When the boy tried haltingly to explain, Barbier stalked out of the room. He angrily refused to even consider making changes.

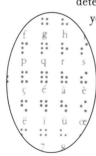

The boy, of course, was Louis Braille. Instead of losing heart, he became determined to develop his ideas on his own. He labored tirelessly for two years to transform night writing into a far simpler system that cut the number of dots in half. He also decided to make them stand for letters instead of sounds. He was just fifteen years old when he completed his system of writing for the blind.

And a new world was revealed to those without sight.

Despite Barbier's refusal to work with him, Braille was always quick to credit him for his role in developing the system that eventually came to be used by blind people worldwide.

> ## " IF I CANNOT DISCOVER A WAY TO READ AND WRITE ... THEN I SHALL KILL MYSELF. "
>
> —LOUIS BRAILLE, IN HIS DIARY

Charles Barbier de la Serre.
Capitaine d'Artillerie.

Braille spent hours every day using a sharp stylus to punch raised dots while he labored to improve Barbier's idea. The tool was remarkably similar to the awl with which Braille accidentally put out one of his eyes when he was just three years old. Infection had set in and soon spread to his other eye, leaving him completely blind.

FIRST COMPUTER

The first computer: invented more than fifty years before the lightbulb.

Railroads were still brand-new in 1822 when a British mathematician named Charles Babbage dreamed up the idea of a mechanical calculator. He called it a "difference engine." Like the railroad, it was designed to operate by steam.

It took Babbage ten years to build just one section of his difference engine. When it was completed, people marveled at its sophistication. But even as he was working on the difference engine he conceived of something even more ambitious: a machine that could be programmed with punch cards to perform even the most complex calculations.

In other words, a mechanical computer.

Babbage made hundreds of drawings outlining his new idea. He envisioned that this "analytical engine" would be about as big and heavy as a small locomotive, containing thousands of finely machined gears. It would be able to add or subtract forty-digit numbers in a few seconds, and multiply similarly large numbers in about two minutes.

Babbage was a bit ahead of his time, since this was a more than hundred years before the first electronic computer was created. Technology was not far enough advanced to create the complex machine. He did, however, develop other more practical things, including something for those newfangled railroad locomotives.

You can still see it on the front of old steam engines.

The cowcatcher.

More than a hundred years later, in 1946, the ENIAC came into existence as the first modern general-purpose computer. Even bigger than the locomotive-sized analytical engine, it contained ten thousand vacuum tubes—and less computing power than a handheld calculator of today.

Babbage was such a perfectionist that every time he started to build the analytical engine, he came up with an idea that would render that version obsolete. Thus it became more and more complex, until it became just about impossible to build.

IN THE NAME OF KALI

A group of hooligans who influenced the way you talk.

In thirteenth-century India, there arose a secret Hindu sect that worshiped Kali, the goddess of destruction. This sect remained a powerful and greatly feared force for more than five hundred years.

Members of the sect lived ordinary lives most of the year, but in the autumn they roamed the countryside in bands, looking for wealthy travelers to kill and sacrifice to their goddess. Their modus operandi was to have one member of the band become friendly with the intended victim while the others awaited an opportunity to strike. They liked to decoy a victim to a secluded spot, sneak up from behind, and strangle him or her with a scarf specially reserved for that purpose.

They became known as the Phansigars ("the stranglers"), but that wasn't their real name.

After the British colonized India, they made a decision to destroy the group. From 1833 to 1837, more than three thousand of its members were arrested. Nearly five hundred were hanged, and thousands more imprisoned for life. The last known member was executed in 1882.

The name of this feared band—the Thugs.

Because the goddess did not like to see blood spilled, victims were usually strangled. But drowning, burning, and poison were also approved methods. The group liked to pick wealthy victims for sacrifice so they could provide a source of revenue as well. Women and musicians, interestingly enough, were considered exempt from attack.

The city of Calcutta (originally Kali-ghata) got its name from Kali. It is the site of a large temple dedicated to the goddess. Kali has always been worshiped by many who were not Thugs, and blood sacrifices are still made to her today. But the victims are usually goats, not people.

This illustration of a band of Thugs (apparently between attacks) appeared in Harper's Weekly in 1857. The accompanying article introduced readers to the tactics of the sect, which often used beautiful women as decoys and schooled its young in the ways of murder.

FAMILY BUSINESS

You may not know Alexander Norris, but what he put together touches every one of us.

In 1837 the United States was in the grip of a financial panic. Markets plunged downward. Hundreds of banks closed their doors. People wondered if the economy would ever right itself again. But in the midst of these hard times, a Midwestern businessman planted a seed that would flower into a multibillion-dollar business.

Alexander Norris had two daughters. One was married to a maker of candles, the other to a maker of soap. Each man's business depended on a steady stream of animal fats. Rather than see his sons-in-law compete for the same raw materials in a depressed economy, Norris urged them to go into business together. Reluctantly, they agreed.

Today, they are recognized around the world for turning animal fat into a fortune. Their small Cincinnati business has become a worldwide powerhouse, with more than 250 brand-name products, from Pepto-Bismol to Pampers. The sons-in-law were named William and James. Their last names?

Procter and Gamble.

In 1879 a P&G workman accidentally left his machine running while he went to lunch, whipping more air than usual into a batch of soap. Soon customers began writing to ask for more of the "soap that floats." The company decided to keep pumping in the extra air, and gave the product a new name: Ivory Soap.

William Procter (left) and James Gamble each put up $3,596.47 to start their new business. Today P&G has annual sales of more than $40 billion, with more than a hundred thousand employees around the world.

This excerpt from an 1837 newspaper describes the panic in terms that are all too familiar to readers of more contemporary news accounts. The economic downturn was so severe that President Martin Van Buren became known as "Martin Van Ruin."

BY THE EXPRESS MAIL.

From the New York Evening Post.

NEW YORK, April 21, 3 p

MONEY MARKETS.—Stocks have receded
ther to-day. We are tired of noting the
it disastrous state of things. Failures are ta
ice every day. Yesterday a new batch
orted. It is impossible to say any thing
ly interest our readers on the subject of the
it unequalled panic; a panic which has sto
the channels of trade, and thrown the poor
anic out of employ. It is an un
lich we state for the i
rs, who m

ONE MAN, ONE VOTE

How a single vote can sometimes make all the difference.

On a sweltering summer afternoon in 1842, Henry Shoemaker was toiling as a hired hand on a farm in Indiana. Suddenly he remembered it was election day, and he had forgotten to vote. He had personally promised his vote to one of the candidates running for state representative, a Democrat named Madison Marsh.

Shoemaker might be forgiven if he had ducked out on his civic duty and broken that promise. But he didn't. He saddled his horse, rode to the polling place, and cast his ballot. As a result, Madison Marsh was elected...*by one vote.*

At that time, state legislators elected U.S. senators. In January of 1843, Marsh and his fellow Indiana lawmakers convened for just such an election. After much maneuvering, Marsh changed his vote on the sixth ballot, electing Democrat Edward Hannegan to the United States Senate...*by one vote.*

Fast-forward to 1846. A sharply divided U.S. Senate was debating whether or not to declare war with Mexico. A caucus vote was deadlocked until the absent Senator Hannegan was called. He cast his vote in favor of war. One of the results of that war was that California changed hands from Mexico to the United States.

Henry Shoemaker had no idea what he was setting in motion that day he went to the polls, never thought that his one vote would make the difference between peace and war. But now that you know, never assume that your *one vote* doesn't count.

Senator Edward Hannegan also cast the deciding vote to give statehood to Texas. So if Henry Shoemaker hadn't cast his vote that day in 1842, it is possible that neither California nor Texas would be part of the United States today.

The reason we know all about Henry Shoemaker's vote is that it was a contested ballot. There wasn't a ticket available listing all the candidates Shoemaker wanted to vote for, so he took out his knife and cut out names from four different tickets in order to cast his ballot. The inspector at the polling place threw out Shoemaker's improvised ticket, and that resulted in a tie. After numerous hearings and lengthy testimony, the vote was allowed and the tie was broken.

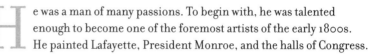

PORTRAIT OF AN INVENTOR

Meet the painter who changed the American landscape—in more ways than one.

He was a man of many passions. To begin with, he was talented enough to become one of the foremost artists of the early 1800s. He painted Lafayette, President Monroe, and the halls of Congress.

He was also America's first camera buff. He fell in love with photography after meeting Louis Daguerre, and was instrumental in introducing the camera to the United States when it was still brand-new.

He was a politician of sorts—although not a very good one. He ran a spectacularly unsuccessful race for mayor of New York City, and almost ran again before friends dissuaded him.

And he had a dark side. He was a zealous anti-Catholic whose passionate writings helped stir up a hatred for immigrants in the United States that would linger for generations.

But we remember him today for quite a different passion—one he labored on for more than a dozen years, suffering ridicule and poverty before it finally captured the attention of the world in 1844 and helped launch an age of instant communication.

Samuel Finley Breese Morse: painter, politician, photographer, fanatic—*and* inventor of the electric telegraph. Truly, an artist with a message.

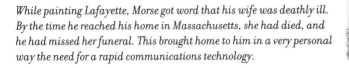

Morse pestered Congress for years to give him money for his telegraph. Many refused to vote for the bill, believing Morse to be either a con man or a lunatic. When he finally got the money he built a forty-mile line between Washington and Baltimore. He convinced the politicians he was onto something when his telegraph carried up-to-the-minute news from the Democratic Party's nominating convention in Baltimore. That was something they could understand.

" WHAT HATH GOD WROUGHT? "

MORSE'S FIRST OFFICIAL
MESSAGE OVER HIS
TELEGRAPH, IN 1844

While painting Lafayette, Morse got word that his wife was deathly ill. By the time he reached his home in Massachusetts, she had died, and he had missed her funeral. This brought home to him in a very personal way the need for a rapid communications technology.

THE CURIOUS CASE OF PHINEAS GAGE

Opening the brain to understanding... literally.

Phineas Gage, a railroad foreman in Cavendish, Vermont, was placing high explosives inside a hole drilled in the rock. But he mistakenly dropped a three-foot-long tamping iron into the hole. It set off an explosion that shot the heavy, inch-thick pole back out the hole and straight through his own head. It entered under his cheekbone and exited through the top of his skull. Gage fell back and went into convulsions.

Everyone was sure that Gage was a goner. But moments later he was up and talking. Expected to die, he confounded doctors by recovering. Something, however, was amiss: Gage had undergone a complete personality change. Gone was the honest, trustworthy, hardworking man that friends had known. The new Gage was vulgar, irresponsible, and prone to bouts of profanity. Fired from his job, he ended up on display in Barnum & Bailey Circus.

After his death, doctors exhumed his remains, and his skull was donated to medical research. In time, his much-studied case helped change the way science looked at how the brain works—providing the first evidence that different regions of the brain might control different things.

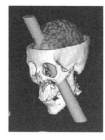

The brain had begun to disclose its secrets—though at great cost to Phineas Gage.

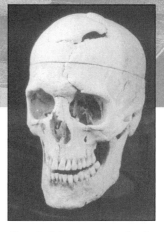

> **THE MOST SINGULAR CIRCUM-STANCE CONNECTED WITH THIS MELANCHOLY AFFAIR IS THAT HE WAS ALIVE AT TWO O'CLOCK THIS AFTERNOON, AND IN FULL POSSESSION OF HIS REASON.**
>
> —*BOSTON POST*, SEPTEMBER 14, THE DAY AFTER THE ACCIDENT

Gage died thirteen years after the accident, penniless and suffering from epilepsy. His skull is now kept at Harvard University.

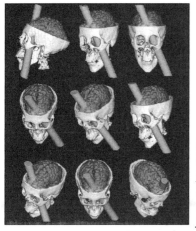

In the early 1990s, two neurobiologists at the University of Iowa used computer graphics and neural imaging techniques to plot the course of the tamping iron as it passed through Gage's skull. They confirmed that it damaged the ventromedial region of the frontal lobes but completely missed that part of the frontal lobes responsible for speech and motor function.

PIN MONEY

An inventive wizard who just couldn't get it right.

In the long history of invention, there is no tale of woe quite like that of Walter Hunt. He was an absolute genius at making things, but an abysmal failure at making money.

In 1834 he invented the first sewing machine in the United States. But there was a depression on, and no one was interested in a machine that would put *more* people out of work. So he didn't bother to file a patent. Bad move. Elias Howe invented and patented a similar machine a few years later, and got rich beyond his wildest dreams.

Hunt also patented the first fountain pen and the first repeating rifle, but failed to turn them into viable products. Others, who did so later, reaped amazing profits.

But the most staggering part of the story was yet to come. One afternoon in 1849 he began playing with a piece of wire. In less than four hours he twisted it into a pin with a spring on one end and a clasp on the other end: the safety pin. A million-dollar idea if ever there was one, and Hunt was quick to patent it. So he became rich—right?

Wrong. Desperate for some quick cash, he sold off the patent rights.

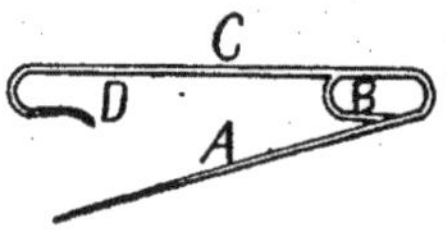

For $100.

Walter Hunt: innovative genius, financial pinhead.

Fig. 2.

Pin.

Patented Apr. 10, 1849.

HE STRUGGLED WITH THAT
MONSTER, THE DOLLAR,
ALL HIS LIFE, IN HOPES OF
MASTERING IT. 99

—*SCIENTIFIC AMERICAN* **OBITUARY**
OF WALTER HUNT BY J. L. KINGSLEY

*Hunt won a measure of fame during his life, and some credit
for inventing the sewing machine. But despite more than twenty-
five patents, he never found that elusive invention that would
bring financial security to his family. At age sixty-three he
died at his workbench while trying to develop a new kind of
diver's apparatus.*

THIS MAGIC MOMENT

*Abracadabra!
How a magician
helped thwart a
rebellion.*

In October of 1856, master magician Jean-Eugène Robert-Houdin came out of retirement for a command performance unlike any before or since. The audience was a gathering of sixty Arab chieftains in the French colony of Algeria, and the purpose was to prevent a rebellion.

Local holy men trying to provoke an uprising against French rule were using tricks to convince their followers that they had supernatural powers. The French hit upon a unique way to undermine their efforts, but it required the help of the man regarded as the finest magician in Europe.

The audience was skeptical, even contemptuous. What could this Frenchman possibly do that compared with their own holy men, who could eat fire and stab themselves without injury? But the old magician rose to the occasion. He asked one member of the audience to shoot him—"Aim straight at my heart," he said. Then he caught the bullet with his hand. He made another member of the audience disappear, and stripped the strength away from a third man. The crowd was seized with fear, and cries of "Satan" were heard. Robert-Houdin had shown himself to be a true sorcerer.

But then he did the unthinkable. He sent out translators to explain how his tricks were done. The chieftains realized their holy men possessed no magic—they were simply performing tricks of their own. For the moment, at least, the threat of rebellion evaporated—as if by magic.

Years after Robert-Houdin's death, his legend so captivated
an up-and-coming magician named Ehrich Weiss that he changed his name—
to Harry Houdini. After achieving fame and fortune of his own, Houdini
became disenchanted with the man who had inspired him, and wrote
a book titled The Unmasking of Robert-Houdin.

66 HE HAS
KNOWN HOW
TO STIR OUR
HEARTS AND
ASTONISH
OUR MINDS. 99

–TESTIMONIAL
PRESENTED BY
ARAB CHIEFTAINS
AFTER THE
PERFORMANCE

Robert-Houdin greatly impressed his audience when he invited a muscular volunteer to lift a metal box, which he
did with ease. The magician then declared: "Behold, you are weaker than a woman. Try now to lift the box."
Muscles taut, eyes bulging, the man lifted with every ounce of strength, but the box wouldn't budge. An assistant
had secretly turned on a powerful electromagnet that held the box to the ground.

NOT WHISTLING "DIXIE"

The most famous song of the South— born and bred in the North.

D ixie," the anthem of the South, was actually written in a New York hotel room by a man from Ohio. The year was 1859, and composer Daniel Decatur Emmett wrote the song on a rainy Sunday afternoon for Bryant's Minstrels, one of the blackfaced minstrel shows popular at the time. It proved to be such a hit that other minstrel shows around the country started using it too.

In 1861 it was played at the inauguration of Jefferson Davis as president of the Confederate States of America. Soon it became the marching song for the Confederate Army. "It is marvelous," wrote one Southern soldier, "with what wildfire rapidity this tune 'Dixie' has spread across the whole South."

This was an outrage to Emmett, a staunch Union supporter. "If I'd known to what use they were going to put my song," he reportedly said, "I'll be damned if I'd have written it."

So Emmett, the creator of "Dixie," was actually a damned Yankee!

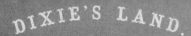

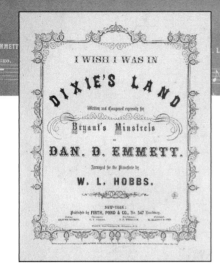

I WISH I WAS IN

DIXIE'S LAND

Written and Composed expressly for

Bryant's Minstrels

DAN. D. EMMETT.

Arranged for the Pianoforte by

W. L. HOBBS.

NEW-YORK:
Published by FIRTH, POND & CO., No 547 Broadway.

> ❝ **IT MADE A TREMENDOUS HIT, AND BEFORE THE END OF THE WEEK EVERYBODY IN NEW YORK WAS WHISTLING IT.** ❞
>
> —DAN EMMETT, ON THE FIRST
> PERFORMANCE OF "DIXIE," IN 1859

The day after Robert E. Lee surrendered at Appomattox, President Lincoln asked a band outside the White House to strike up "Dixie." "I have always thought 'Dixie' one of the best tunes I ever heard," Lincoln said. "Our adversaries over the way attempted to appropriate it, but we have fairly captured it."

A contemporary of Stephen Foster, Dan Emmett wrote two other minstrel songs that became American classics, "Jimmy Crack Corn" and "Old Dan Tucker." After the Civil War he came to cherish the South's love of "Dixie." In 1895, at age eighty, he made a farewell tour and sang the song to standing ovations across the region.

PONY EXPRESS

*How a failed
business venture
created an
American legend.*

As kids, many of us thrilled to the adventures and romance of the Pony Express. Daring riders galloping thousands of miles across the dangerous Western plains, braving Indians, bandits, and natural hazards to bring the mail from Saint Joseph, Missouri, all the way to California in just ten days.

But guess what? The real Pony Express was a disaster: an impractical, money-losing business that went bankrupt in little more than a year and cost investors nearly a quarter of a million dollars.

Begun in 1860 with eighty riders and five hundred horses, it was doomed almost before it began by the construction of the transcontinental telegraph. Once the telegraph was completed, in August of 1861, the Pony Express was obsolete. It went out of business two months later.

During its brief life, however, it captured the country's imagination. And while the business went belly-up…the legend rode off into the sunset.

Sending a message by Pony Express wasn't cheap. A half-ounce letter cost $5. That's the equivalent of more than $90 today. Once the telegraph was built, it was both quicker and cheaper, at least for short messages.

> ## "THREE CHEERS FOR THE FIRST OVERLAND PASSAGE OF THE UNITED STATES MAIL!"
>
> —MAYOR JEFF THOMPSON OF SAINT JOSEPH, MISSOURI, ON THE FIRST DAY OF PONY EXPRESS SERVICE

One young fellow who took up the challenge of being a Pony Express rider was a fourteen-year-old Kansas boy named William Cody. Buffalo Bill, as he later became known, turned his western experiences into a famous Wild West Show that toured the United States and Europe for decades.

Riders had to weigh less than 125 pounds, and many were young boys. The riders changed horses every ten to fifteen miles to keep up a steady pace. This young man's name is Frank E. Webner.

TELEPHONE TALE

*Being first doesn't
always mean
being famous.*

Alexander Graham Bell invented the telephone in 1876—right? Well, actually, a German schoolteacher managed to do it fifteen years before Bell, but he didn't have very good PR.

In 1860 Philip Reis rigged up what he described as an "artificial ear." This crude instrument was built from an improbable assortment of items: a violin, a knitting needle, an ear carved in wood, even a piece of sausage. "I succeeded in inventing an apparatus by which...one can reproduce sounds of all kinds at any desired distance....I named the instrument [the] 'telephone.'"

It worked—but poorly. So Reis kept tinkering with it. He hooked up a wire between his workshop and the school, which convinced his students that he was using the telephone to eavesdrop on them. He worked on his telephone for several years and his models became more and more sophisticated.

Eventually Reis sent some improved models of his telephone to scientists around the world. They could transmit music fairly well, but speech came out garbled at best. "Single words...were perceptible indistinctly," said one listener. Nobody seemed very impressed.

Most scientists at the time regarded the Reis telephone as little more than a toy. Crushed, he abandoned work on it, and died of tuberculosis in 1874. Two years later, Alexander Graham Bell filed the patent that earned him the glory and financial rewards of telephone invention.

Alexander Graham Bell didn't set out to invent a telephone. He was trying to build a better telegraph that could send multiple messages down the same wire. But once he realized he could make a telephone, he could think of nothing else.

Bell's great competitor in telephone invention was Elisha Gray, whose application for a telephone patent was filed just hours after Bell's. At the time, Gray didn't seem to understand what he'd lost out on. "The talking telegraph is a beautiful thing from a scientific point of view," he wrote in 1876. "But if you look at in a business light, it is of no importance."

THE GUN MEANT TO SAVE LIVES

A Civil War doctor tries to save lives in a most unusual way.

I n the opening year of the War Between the States, an Ohio doctor found himself horrified at the growing number of young men whose lives were being snuffed out. He noted that more men were falling from disease than from enemy bullets. That gave him an idea.

"It occurred to me," he wrote later, "that if I could invent a machine—a gun—which could by its rapidity of fire, enable one man do as much battle duty as a hundred, that it would supercede the necessity of large armies, and consequently, exposure to battle and disease [would] be greatly diminished." In other words, he hoped that by inventing a better gun, he could save lives.

He tied six gun barrels around a revolving shaft and built a device to fire and reload them automatically. His machine gun could spit out 350 bullets per minute, more than one hundred times what a standard-issue rifle could do. By late 1862 his weapon was ready for action, and if it had gone into production then, it could have had a dramatic impact on the war. But a fire burned down the factory and all his plans, forcing him to start over.

His gun finally saw battle late in the war and proved devastating when Union soldiers turned it upon the enemy. After the war, the U.S. Army ordered a hundred of Dr. Richard Gatling's new guns, and soon armies around the world were buying them. Machine guns have gone on to become a most efficient means of killing. The thought they might save lives? Long since buried—along with Dr. Gatling.

In 1874 Gatling came out with a compact "Camel" gun, designed to be mounted on a small tripod or a camel saddle. But the name was more a marketing ploy than a practical application.

Compliments of R.J. Gatling
ford, May 1st 1893.

Gatling guns were state-of-the-art until after the turn of the century. Even today they are far from obsolete. A new generation of the gun is being used in many modern military aircraft. The weapons are capable of firing more than four thousand rounds per minute.

THIS BOX CONTAINS
ONE GATLING GUN,
Calibre .30, Model 1897.

1 Crank Handle and Pin.
1 Pointing Lever,
1 Axis Pin, Washer and Nut,
1 Binder Box, Plate, Screw, Pin,
    Washer and Key,
2 Guide Ways,
1 Shell Driver,
1 Wiping Rod (Brass).

1 Lock Screw Driver,
1 T Screw Driver,
1 Small Screw Driver,
1 Rear Guide Nut Wrench,
1 Cascable Wrench,
1 Lever Axis Pin Nut Wrench,
1 Pin Wrench,
1 Drift.

MANUFACTURED BY
Colt's Patent Fire Arms Mfg. Co., Hartford, Conn.

THREE CIGARS

Think how different things would be if the South had won the Civil War. It might have happened... but for three cigars.

In September of 1862, Confederate general Robert E. Lee seized the initiative and invaded the North. It was a critical time in the war. If Lee could win a decisive victory, European nations might recognize the Confederacy, and the war would for all intents and purposes be over—with the triumphant South an independent nation.

Chasing Lee was General George McClellan, one of the most overcautious officers ever to wear Union blue. His response to Lee's bold moves was slow and hesitant. As his army moved slowly through Maryland, searching for Lee's troops, McClellan agonized over what he should do.

Fate intervened when an Indiana regiment stopped for a rest in a field occupied by Confederates a few days before. Three soldiers sprawled out on the ground noticed an envelope lying in the grass. Inside were three cigars wrapped in a piece of paper. Delighted, the soldiers decided to split the cigars—and then one of them thought to look at the paper.

His curiosity changed history.

He had found what a Confederate officer had lost—a copy of the marching orders for Lee's army, telling where the Confederates were headed and what they had planned. Galvanized by this captured information, McClellan promptly went on the attack.

The result: the Confederates were turned back at the Battle of Antietam, on the bloodiest single day in American history.

All because of three cigars.

More than five thousand Americans were killed at Antietam. Nearly twenty thousand more were wounded. Among those wounded was Corporal Barton W. Mitchell, one of the three soldiers who brought on the battle by finding the cigars.

66 **HERE IS A PAPER WITH WHICH IF I CANNOT WHIP BOBBY LEE I WILL BE WILLING TO GO HOME.** 99

—GENERAL GEORGE MCCLELLAN

This is the paper found by the soldiers, Special Orders 191. They were written out by Lee's assistant adjutant general, R. H. Chilton. By sheer coincidence, one of the Union officers who examined the orders happened to know Chilton before the war, and was able to verify that it was his handwriting—thus convincing General McClellan the document was genuine.

AMAZING FAX

If you think of the fax machine as a modern convenience, consider this: the first one was invented more than 140 years ago.

Giovanni Caselli was a priest, but his neighbors in Florence thought of him as a bit of a mad scientist. He was eternally tinkering with things, and his home was always filled with junk.

The telegraph was the hot new technology of the moment, and Caselli wondered if it was possible to send *pictures* over telegraph wires. He went to work in 1857, and over the course of six years perfected what he called the "pantelegraph." It was the world's first practical fax machine. Standing six feet tall and made up of swinging pendulums, batteries, and wires, it worked by passing an electrical current through an image. The signal was sent to a receiver that translated it onto a piece of treated paper.

Emperor Napoleon III of France was so impressed with Caselli's work that he authorized use of the machine on French telegraph lines. By 1868 the pantelegraph was transmitting as many as 110 faxes per hour. But it was viewed as a novelty, not a necessity. When Prussian troops invaded France in 1870, the service was interrupted, never to be resumed again. It was another hundred years before the modern fax machine suddenly became indispensable.

In addition to being a scientist, Caselli was also a hotheaded political radical. His views had so angered the church that he was actually living in exile at the time he invented the pantelegraph.

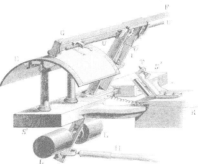

On the transmitting end, a stylus attached to a pendulum would swing back and forth over the original. When it touched the ink it would send an electrical signal to a synchronized stylus passing over chemically treated paper on the other end. This caused the paper to change color wherever electricity touched it. The result was an exact copy.

THE ACTOR AND THE SON

*One brother
saves a life—
the other takes one.*

One of America's most famous actors stood on a train platform in Jersey City. He was among a crowd of people about to get on board a train. As the crowd pressed forward to enter one of the coaches, the train unexpectedly started with a jolt, rolling a few feet before it stopped. The actor saw a young man lose his balance, and begin to fall helplessly between the platform and the moving car.

Thinking quickly, the actor reached down and grabbed the young fellow by the collar, pulling him to safety. The grateful young man recognized his celebrity savior, "whose face was of course well known to me, and I expressed my gratitude to him, and in doing so, called him by name."

It is only later that the two men recognized the haunting irony.

The actor was Edwin Booth. His younger brother, John Wilkes Booth, assassinated President Lincoln the following spring. And the young man whose life he saved?

Robert Todd Lincoln—Abraham Lincoln's son.

Famed for his staging of Shakespearean tragedies, Booth earned great public acclaim by performing Hamlet for a record-breaking one hundred consecutive nights on Broadway, in 1864. President Lincoln saw both Edwin Booth and his brother perform on stage.

With a helping hand from Edwin Booth, Robert Todd Lincoln became the only one of President Lincoln's four children who survived to adulthood. He later became secretary of war and president of the Pullman Railroad Company.

THE BEGINNING AND THE END

The Civil War started in his backyard and ended in his front parlor.

In July of 1861, the first major battle of the Civil War was fought in Manassas, Virginia. The Battle of Bull Run was a confused and bloody clash that shocked the nation with its carnage.

Wilmer McLean owned a plantation on the edge of the battlefield. It was so close to the fighting that a shell pierced the kitchen wall. That was too close a call as far as McLean was concerned. He moved his family to a remote Virginia town "where the sound of battle would never reach them."

But in the end, the war caught up to them.

Four years later, Robert E. Lee led the weary remnants of his Confederate Army into that very town—Appomattox Courthouse. On April 9, 1865, he decided his men could fight no more, and sought a meeting with General Grant to negotiate terms of surrender. One of Lee's aides selected a place for the two men to meet. It was just by a quirk of fate that the place he picked was the front room of Wilmer McLean's new home.

Dressed in his fanciest uniform, Lee projected nothing but cool while meeting with Grant. But in truth he was so agitated that he considered charging enemy lines on his horse that morning, so that he might be gunned down by Union sharpshooters and thus avoid the humiliation of surrendering.

I WAS THE ALPHA AND THE OMEGA OF THIS CONTEST.

—WILMER MCLEAN

After the surrender, the McLean house quickly fell victim to tourists and profiteers. Union officers snapped up all the furniture to sell as souvenirs. When McLean tried to resist, they threw money on the floor and took what they wanted. McLean himself began charging admission to curious soldiers. Later, a speculator bought the house and dismantled it in the hopes of making it a tourist attraction in Washington, D.C.

QWERTY...

The indispensable part of your computer that is more than a century old.

The modern typewriter was born in the back of Kleinsteuber's Machine Shop in Milwaukee. That's where Christopher Sholes took some piano wire and a telegraph key and built a crude typing device in 1868. It could type only one letter, a rather fuzzy-looking *w*, but it was still pretty amazing for its time. Sholes and his partners designed a more ambitious model with all the letters in the alphabet.

The typewriter had a problem, though. Try to type quickly on it, and the type bars banged into one another and got stuck. The solution to that problem resulted in the keyboard we know today.

Sholes consulted with an educator who helped him analyze the most common pairings of letters in the English language. He then split up those letters so that their type bars were farther apart and less likely to jam. That in turn dictated the layout of the keyboard—known as QWERTY, for the first five letters in the upper row. In a manner of speaking, he slowed down the typists to prevent jamming, and thus speed up the typing.

In 1873 the Sholes & Glidden Type Writer became the first to be mass-produced, and its keyboard layout was soon standard on all typewriters. Other keyboard layouts have been created since, such as the Blickensderfer Scientific and the Dvorak, and some are demonstrably more efficient, but the original continues to thrive. It is a telling illustration of the power of inertia and the reward of being first.

Sholes's single-key prototype.

> ## A MACHINE TO SUPERSEDE THE PEN FOR ALL KINDS OF WRITING

—1876 ADVERTISEMENT FOR TYPEWRITER

The original Sholes & Glidden typed only capitals and was designed in an awkward fashion that prevented the typist from looking at the paper while typing. Ads trumpeted its value to clergymen and lawyers, but it sold quite poorly at first. One reason: it was expensive. It cost $125, the equivalent of more than $1,700 today.

SECRET SUBWAY

*If you ride the
A train, it's hard
to believe that New
York's first subway
was built in secret.*

In 1912, construction workers digging a new subway line stumbled upon something almost shocking: a fully preserved station they never knew existed. It was the brainchild of Alfred Beach, editor of *Scientific American*. In the 1860s he became appalled by New York's traffic. His innovative solution: build an air-powered train underground.

The most powerful person in New York, William Marcy "Boss" Tweed, was dead set against the idea. To outsmart Tweed and gain public support, Beach decided to build a 312-foot-long subway beneath Broadway *in total secret*. Furthermore, he had the gall to run it right under City Hall. He concocted a clever cover story, claiming that he was building a pneumatic tube to carry messages between buildings. To keep his secret, all the work was done at night. Dirt was carried out through a nearby basement, and construction materials came in the same way.

In February of 1870 he threw the doors open to an amazed public, who were delighted by the luxuriously appointed station and the clean running train. But Tweed was outraged, and fought tooth and nail against Beach's plan to expand the subway. Eventually Beach got the permission he needed from the governor, but a financial panic killed investor interest. Beach reluctantly sealed the tunnel up, and it was soon forgotten. New Yorkers would have to wait until the twentieth century to commute underground.

The train was powered by a fifty-ton fan nicknamed the Western Tornado. The New York Times *called Beach's project "certainly the most novel, if not the most successful, enterprise that New York has seen for many a day."* But some prominent people opposed it because they feared that an underground train would undermine buildings on the street above.

> ## A TUBE, A CAR, A REVOLVING FAN! LITTLE MORE IS REQUIRED!

—ALFRED BEACH

New Yorkers gasped at the luxury of the station. Frescoes lined the walls, goldfish swam in a sparkling fountain, and a grand piano provided background music as passengers lounged in easy chairs. The train operated for a year, and more than four hundred thousand people paid admission just to see it.

NOT THE CHICAGO FIRE

Discover the amazing coincidence behind the deadliest fire in U.S. history.

Maybe you've heard this story. On the evening of October 8, 1871, a small fire started near the O'Learys' barn on the south side of Chicago.

Strong winds whipped it into the Great Chicago Fire. It raged through the city for thirty-one hours, killing 250 people, destroying 18,000 buildings, and leaving 100,000 homeless. Damage was estimated at $200 million. The devastation was immense.

But it wasn't the deadliest fire in U.S. history.

That dubious honor goes to a frightening blaze that killed more than a thousand people in northern Wisconsin, in and around the lumber town of Peshtigo. This howling forest fire jumped from tree to tree so fast that it was impossible to run away from, and it simply incinerated Peshtigo and other towns in its path.

But hardly anyone's ever heard of the Great Peshtigo Fire. A case of bad timing, perhaps. It took place 250 miles north of the Chicago fire...on the very same night.

> # FORTY MILES AWAY WE STILL SAW THE BRILLIANT FLAMES LOOMING ABOVE THE DOOMED CITY.
>
> —JOHN R. CHAPIN, EYEWITNESS TO
> THE GREAT CHICAGO FIRE

"It was about ten o'clock when we entered into the river," said the Reverend Peter Pernin of Peshtigo. "Once in water up to our necks, I thought we would at least be safe from the fire, but it was not so; the flames darted over the river as they did over the land, the air was full of them, or rather the air itself was on fire."

In Chicago, as well, residents thought the river meant safety, and thousands fled across the bridges. But here, too, the fire jumped the river and kept on going.

MRS. SATAN

*They called this
devil-may-care
presidential
candidate
Mrs. Satan.*

In May of 1872, the Equal Rights Party nominated Victoria Woodhull for president, before women even had the right to vote. She was a thirty-three-year-old social reformer who was also an outspoken advocate of free love. She told reporters it was a sure cure for immorality.

The flamboyant Woodhull took great delight in defying convention and breaking down barriers. A self-proclaimed clairvoyant who performed in her youth at carnivals, Woodhull and her sister achieved fame as America's first (and only) female stockbrokers, and published their own crusading newspaper.

When critics contended that Woodhull's promiscuity made her little better than a prostitute, she turned the tables: her paper accused one of the most famous ministers of the day, Henry Ward Beecher, of practicing sexual infidelity while preaching against it. Woodhull knew what she was talking about—she herself had been one of Beecher's lovers. The incendiary charges ignited a national sex scandal. Woodhull was jailed for pornography, and cartoonist Thomas Nast labeled her "Mrs. Satan."

The fact is, this extraordinary woman eventually married not the devil, but an English banker. The scandal stirred up so much hatred she fled the country. Leaving the tumult behind her, she created a new persona and lived out the second half of her life as a respected member of the British upper class.

Woodhull had only scorn for those who "preach against free love openly, and practice it secretly." She went after Beecher to illustrate what she considered to be a national double standard that gave men sexual freedom but denied it to women. Throughout the ensuing scandal, Beecher never denied her accusations.

Cornelius Vanderbilt fell under the spell of Woodhull and her sister, providing financial backing for their stock brokerage. The women played up to their reputation as spiritualists, claiming their stock picks came to them while in a trance. Newspapers referred to them as "the Bewitching Brokers."

CARTOON CHARACTERS

How one man's imagination turned politics into an animal farm.

I n the years between the Civil War and the turn of the century, Thomas Nast was the nation's most influential political cartoonist. In fact, the influence of his powerful cartoons is still felt today.

Nast, a die-hard Republican, liked to use the jackass to portray Democratic policies he considered hotheaded or downright stubborn. When others picked up on the symbol, the Democrats tried to make the best of it, portraying themselves as donkeys, not asses.

A few weeks before election day in 1874, Nast drew a cartoon for *Harper's Magazine* in which he used a rogue elephant to represent Republican voters he felt were being panicked by phony charges from the Democrats. The cartoon was meant as a rebuke, but the idea of a pachyderm representing the GOP soon took on a life of its own.

The issues and controversies of those days have long since faded, but the elephant and donkey have proved amazingly resilient.

The German-born artist also helped shape our image of Santa Claus. Trying to capture the "jolly old elf" of Clement Moore's poem "A Visit from St. Nicholas" (" 'Twas the night before Christmas, and all through the house ... "), he created the face of Santa we've come to take for granted.

Nast, seen here at the height of his popularity, did more than just shape American popular culture. He may well have influenced the style of artist Vincent van Gogh. Van Gogh systematically collected Nast's work, even saving a collection of Nast illustrations in a bound volume for reference.

1880

LAND WAR

Meet an English landlord who unwittingly gave his name to a revolutionary form of protest.

Irish tenant farmers were outraged over high rents set by their English landlords. So in 1880, they organized. They called themselves the Land League, and their movement swept the nation overnight. Along the way it gave birth to a new tactic that became a staple of nonviolent organizations down through the decades.

One of the first and most notorious targets was a British estate manager in County Mayo. The Land League demanded that he reduce his rents because of a bad harvest. His response was less than conciliatory—he brought in constables to evict his tenants.

The Land League responded in a manner that would soon be the talk of the world. Local residents refused to sell him supplies, pick his crops, or even talk to him. Instead they hooted and jeered at him whenever he appeared in public. His nerve soon broke, and he fled the country.

The estate manager is now long dead, but his name lives on, now attached to the revolutionary tactic first used against him.

Charles Cunningham *Boycott.*

> ## NO LABORER DARED TO WORK FOR HIM, NO TRADESMAN TO SERVE HIM WITH GOODS.
>
> —*HARPER'S WEEKLY.*
> DECEMBER 1880

Captain Boycott's name entered the language with astonishing speed. The tactic was introduced against him in September. By November newspaper stories in Britain and America already referred to it as "Boycotting."

Boycott was compelled to use his own wife and daughters to harvest the estate's crops under the watchful eye of the local constabulary. He left for England shortly thereafter.

WHO KILLED GARFIELD?

President James Garfield: shot by a lawyer, killed by his doctors.

In July of 1881, President Garfield set out for his college reunion. But as he walked through Washington's railroad station he was gunned down by Charles Guiteau, a mentally unbalanced lawyer who was angry with Garfield for denying him a diplomatic post.

Doctors spent the next eighty days trying to remove the bullet. Dr. Willard Bliss stuck a probe into the wound, creating a path that misled other doctors. Then he compounded his error by inserting an unwashed finger in the hole, introducing infection. Another doctor stuck his hand in wrist-deep and accidentally punctured the liver. Together the sixteen doctors who poked and prodded Garfield turned a three-inch hole into a twenty-inch infected canal.

The president lingered on in great pain throughout the summer, finally dying on September 14. An autopsy revealed that the bullet was lodged in a spot that was *not* life threatening.

Garfield would have survived...if only they'd left him alone.

Dr. Bliss had the dubious distinction of being the only doctor attending the deaths of both President Garfield and President Abraham Lincoln. He and the other doctors who treated Garfield were publicly accused of malpractice, and Bliss later apologized.

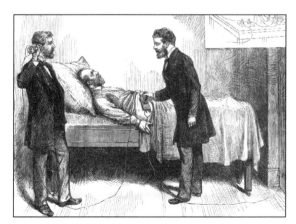

Guiteau made the doctors' incompetence the centerpiece of his defense, saying he didn't kill Garfield: "The doctors did that. I simply shot at him." Correct as he might have been, he was nonetheless convicted and hanged.

LADIES ONLY

TICKET OFFICE

66 **ASSASSINATION CAN NO MORE BE GUARDED AGAINST THAN DEATH BY LIGHTNING; AND IT IS BEST NOT TO WORRY ABOUT EITHER.** 99

—PRESIDENT JAMES GARFIELD

Even Alexander Graham Bell got into the act, devising a crude metal detector to locate the bullet. It worked with every patient he tested it on, but failed miserably with the president. Bell was unaware that Garfield was resting on a coil spring mattress—brand-new at the time—and the coils foiled the metal detector.

DOCTOR OF REASON

The curious case of the doctor who gave birth to a superstar.

Dr. Joseph Bell was a professor of medicine at the University of Edinburgh. His students were amazed by his astonishing powers of observation. He seemed able to determine what patients did for a living, or what illness they might have, simply by glancing in their direction. One time he concluded that a patient had walked across a golf course on the way to the doctor, simply by looking at his shoes. Another time he was able to determine not only that a patient had been in the army, but also which regiment he served in.

One of Bell's students was particularly impressed with his teacher's abilities. He filled up notebooks with examples of what he called Bell's "eerie trick of spotting details." The student eventually went into practice himself outside London. When business was slow he filled his spare moments by writing stories.

He took Dr. Bell's powers of perception, and gave them to a character of his own making—a character who made the young doctor, Arthur Conan Doyle, famous the world over. And so the professor who made even the most complex diagnosis seem "elementary" became the inspiration for fiction's greatest detective.

Sherlock Holmes.

Once it was revealed that Bell was the model for the great detective, the Edinburgh doctor found himself deluged with fan mail and interview requests. He relished the attention, but sometimes found it tiresome. "I am haunted by my double," he wrote a friend.

❝ IT IS MOST CERTAINLY TO YOU THAT I OWE SHERLOCK HOLMES. ❞

—ARTHUR CONAN DOYLE
TO JOE BELL

Arthur Conan Doyle was quick to credit Bell with the uncanny powers of deduction that were Sherlock Holmes's trademark: "I do not think that his analytical work is in the least an exaggeration of some of the effects I have seen you produce." Bell himself took a more modest view of his role: "Dr. Conan Doyle, by his imaginative genius, made a great deal out of very little."

MARKETING THE ELECTRIC CHAIR

The bitter corporate rivalry that helped power an execution.

On August 6, 1890, convicted murderer William Kemmler was strapped into an electric chair. He was about to become the first man executed by electrocution, thanks in part to one of the most macabre chapters in the history of marketing.

After the invention of the first practical lightbulb, everyone wanted electricity in their homes, and two men were engaged in a fierce battle to control the market. Thomas Edison favored using direct current, known as DC. George Westinghouse thought alternating current, or AC, was superior. Their conflict became known as the War of the Currents.

At first Edison's DC took the lead, thanks in part to Edison's great reputation. But then AC started catching up, because it was easier and cheaper to transmit across long distances. Edison decided to discredit AC by proving how dangerous it was. Not only did he issue dire warnings to the public; he also suggested to the state of New York that it use a Westinghouse AC generator as a humane method of execution. If it used AC, said Edison, it should produce "instantaneous death."

Westinghouse was outraged and refused to provide a generator. But Edison and his allies managed to procure one, and so it was that AC powered the killing chair.

Edison won the battle, but Westinghouse won the war. The advantages of AC were too hard to ignore, and it became the household standard.

Edison and his colleagues tried to come up with a suitably scary word for death by electricity. Edison suggested "ampermort" and "dynamort," while an associate thought "electricide" would be just right. One of Edison's lawyers had a more ghoulish suggestion: "Why not speak hereafter of a criminal as being 'westinghoused,' or as being ...'condemned to the westinghouse?'"

> ## STRONG MEN FAINTED AND FELL ON THE FLOOR. 99

—NEW YORK HERALD,
DESCRIBING THE FIRST USE
OF THE ELECTRIC CHAIR

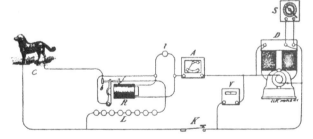

Edison let his lab be used for secret experiments in which more than 50 dogs and cats were shocked to death with AC. Then he and his allies went public, holding demonstrations in which they electrocuted dogs, horses, and calves to show both how dangerous AC was and how effective it would be in an electric chair.

ANNIE AND THE KAISER

A single gunshot that could have prevented the War to End All Wars.

Annie Oakley was nervous. Just moments before, while she was performing her trick-shooting act before a crowd of thousands, a prominent local citizen had surprised her by stepping out of the audience. Gesturing emphatically, he challenged Annie to shoot the ashes off his cigarette as he was smoking it.

As Annie told the story later, Wild West bravado compelled her to accept. After all, she had done this trick before. But his fame unnerved her. Anxiously, she paced off the distance, regretting the whiskey had she consumed the night before. The man drew a cigarette from his gold case and lit it with a flourish. Hesitating only a moment, Annie took aim and fired.

The bullet knocked the ashes off the cigarette, and the crowd roared with delight. The show was in Berlin. The man? None other than the newly crowned monarch: the young Kaiser Wilhelm of Germany.

Had the bullet strayed off course, the belligerent ruler who played a major role in launching World War I might never have had the chance. It was a moment Annie never forgot.

During World War I, Annie's husband, Frank Butler, told reporters that he had written the Kaiser (now the hated enemy), saying Annie would like the chance to take a second shot at him. Wilhelm wisely never replied.

> ## IF I SHOT THE KAISER, I MIGHT HAVE SAVED THE LIVES OF SEVERAL MILLIONS OF SOLDIERS.
>
> —ANNIE OAKLEY

In 1898, on the eve of the Spanish-American War, Annie wrote to President William McKinley offering to put at his disposal "a company of fifty lady sharpshooters." Annie promised that each member of the company would provide her own rifle and ammunition. Nothing ever came of the offer.

REVOLUTION IN A CEREAL BOWL

Meet the man whose passion for digestion transformed breakfast.

In the 1890s people flocked to the Battle Creek Sanitarium in Michigan. They came to partake of the wisdom being dispensed by America's newest health guru.

He was a medical doctor down on the American diet. He called modern cooking "the greatest bane of civilization." A charismatic speaker and author, he told audiences that the key to human happiness lay in the digestive tract. Indigestion, he wrote, "is responsible for more deaths than all other causes combined."

The San, as the sanitarium was called, served up healthy low-calorie meals, although sometimes they were a bit short on taste. But the doctor worried about what would happen to his patients' eating habits when they returned home. He began experimenting in the kitchen to develop a low-calorie, ready-to-eat breakfast food that he could sell by mail order. With the help of his wife and brother, he came up with a brand-new health food that would one day adorn breakfast tables across the nation.

The food: toasted corn flakes. The name of the doctor behind it: John Harvey Kellogg.

Always concerned with the state of his digestive track and bowels, John Harvey Kellogg had an enema administered to himself every morning. He also claimed to have been celibate through more than forty years of marriage. His regimen seemed to keep him healthy—he lived into his nineties.

the market. But they imitate
clusively to the original Toasted
for it when you buy. Get it at

-But They Can't Use This Signature

W. K. Kellogg

On a Package

Sanitas TOASTED CORN FLAKES

This is your guide— your absolute protection in getting the
ORIGINAL — GENUINE
TOASTED CORN FLAKES

Corn flakes were just another mail-order product until Kellogg's brother Will Keith took over the food business, left the San, and started his own company. W. K. had a flair for marketing. One famous ad asked people not to buy the new product, because there wasn't enough available. As a result it flew off the shelves.

The San attracted thousands seeking better health through clean living. It offered "daily cold water and air baths" accompanied by "frequent changes of underwear." People who went there were proud to wear the title Battle Freaks.

OF FLASHLIGHTS AND MODEL TRAINS

The man who gives up a fortune... to play with his trains.

Illuminated flowerpots. That was the thing—thought Joshua L. Cowen—that was surely going to make him a fortune. Though only in his twenties, Cowen was already an experienced inventor. His latest design consisted of a slender metal tube with batteries in the middle and a lightbulb on the end. He figured you could stick one in a flowerpot so that it would illuminate the plant in a restaurant or store display.

It did wind up making a fortune, but not for Cowen. The problem was that other people were coming up with the idea of a battery-operated light at the same time, and everybody was hiring lawyers and threatening to sue. It all became a bit much for Cowen, so he signed his rights over to a business associate named Conrad Hubert. Hubert wasn't interested in flower-pots—he wanted to put the small battery-operated light into people's *hands*. He started the American Eveready Company, and raked in millions selling flashlights and batteries.

But don't feel too bad for Joshua L. Cowen. He always had a passion for railroads, and after designing a tiny electric motor for a miniature fan, he realized it was just the right size to power a miniature train. He started selling model trains by catalog as eyecatching displays for shopwindows—he probably figured they were at least as good as illuminated flowerpots. Customers fell in love with the motorized models and began snapping them up as Christmas gifts for their children.

The *L* in Joshua L. Cowen's name stood for Lionel. The rest is model train history.

WITNESSES:

Cowen's lifelong interest in model trains began at age seven, when he carved a locomotive out of wood, then tried installing a tiny steam engine of his own design. It exploded.

FIG.1.

Just to muddy the waters a bit, Cowen's first invention was called a "flash-lamp." It looked like a flashlight, but instead of lighting a bulb at the end, it ignited flash powder, which photographers used to take pictures. The navy thought it would make a great fuse for mines—which wasn't what Cowen had in mind—but he liked it fine when the government bought ten thousand of them.

THE ELECTION THAT KILLED

The hotly contested election that wound up killing the voters.

In May of 1902, election season was heating up on the Caribbean island of Martinique. So was the island volcano, Mount Pelée. It was belching smoke and fire, and otherwise making a nuisance of itself. In the city of Saint-Pierre, at the foot of the volcano, residents regarded the fiery peak with mounting concern.

The governor of Martinique, however, was more worried about the upcoming election than he was about the volcano. Governor Louis Mouttet feared that a panic would hurt the candidates of the ruling Progressive Party. So he directed the editor of the local paper to downplay the danger of an eruption. He set up roadblocks to prevent people from leaving the city. He suppressed telegrams warning of the danger. And in a grand gesture, he paid a visit to Saint-Pierre three days before the election to assure everyone that things were just fine.

The following morning, at 8 A.M., Pelée erupted. A cloud of superheated gas and ash more than one thousand degrees centigrade hurtled through the town at nearly a hundred miles per hour. It didn't distinguish between political parties, but killed the governor and thirty thousand others in less than two minutes.

There were only two survivors. Ironically, one was a prisoner in an underground cell who was scheduled for execution the next day.

Governor Mouttet said he was covering up warnings about the volcano because they "could create a state of false fear and pessimism." It apparently never occurred to him that the fear could be justified.

Auguste Ciparis, the condemned man who survived the eruption, was lucky enough to have his sentence commuted. He spent years traveling with the Barnum & Bailey Circus in a replica of his cell.

" THIS DATE SHOULD BE WRITTEN IN BLOOD. "

—AN EYEWITNESS TO
THE DEVASTATION

The searing cloud of ash that descended on the city was hot enough to melt glass and metal. All that was left in the beautiful harbor city was smoldering ruins.

THE ICE CREAM CONE COMETH

The century-old controversy about the cook behind the cone.

It happened on a stifling summer's day at the 1904 Saint Louis World's Fair. Ernest Hamwi, an immigrant from Syria, was having no luck selling hot Persian waffles to the sweltering crowds. But at the next booth, Arno Fornachau was dishing out ice cream that was selling like, well, hotcakes. Suddenly, Arnold ran out of plates. *Sacré bleu!* What to do?

Ernest had a flash of inspiration. He rolled a cone out of a waffle and offered it as a substitute. Voilà! The ice cream cone was born.

Well, that's the version backed by the International Ice Cream Association. But here's where the story gets sticky. At least half a dozen vendors at the fair claimed *they* actually deserved the credit. Their descendants still carry on a spirited argument about it today.

So what's the real scoop? It's safe to say that the World's Fair Cornucopia, as it was first known, was born at the fair one day and quickly copied by dozens of others eager to get in on a good thing. When the fair was over people took the idea back home and it became a coast-to-coast hit. Today one-third of all ice cream is licked off cones. They are one of America's favorite summer treats—no argument about that.

Fair-goers in Saint Louis delighted by America's newest taste treat.

The family of Charles Menches, another food vendor at the fair, says he invented the ice cream cone when he wrapped a homemade waffle around a wooden fig used to split tent rope. Menches and his brother also laid claim to inventing the hamburger at a county fair in Hamburg, New York, in 1885. The family is involved in the restaurant business to this day.

DIAMOND IN THE ROUGH

The extraordinary history of the world's largest diamond.

In 1905 the superintendent of a South African diamond mine was conducting a routine inspection when he stumbled upon a stone as large as his fist. It was so big that at first he assumed it was a piece of glass planted there as a joke.

But this was no joke. In fact, it was the largest diamond ever discovered, weighing 3,106 carats. Named the Cullinan diamond (after the chairman of the company), it was purchased by the Transvaal Colony, which decided to give it to Britain's King Edward VII as a token of loyalty.

When it came time for the stone to leave the country, armed guards carried a package aboard a steamer, deposited it in the captain's safe, and stood watch over it day and night. What they didn't know was that they were guarding a decoy! Amazingly enough, the real diamond was sent by registered mail, and arrived in the mailroom at Buckingham Palace a month later.

Joseph Asscher, the foremost diamond cutter of his day, spent months studying the stone from every angle to determine where he should make the first cut. A mistake could ruin everything. When he was finally ready, he inserted a blade and struck it with a mallet. The blade shattered! After he succeeded in making the first cut with a new blade, his nerves got the better of him and he fell into a dead faint. Once he revived, it took him another thirty-eight days to cut it into nine major stones and nearly one hundred smaller ones.

All the stones remain in the possession of Britain's royal family. The largest of them, known as the Greater Star of Africa, today adorns the royal scepter. It is the largest cut diamond in the world—weighing 530 carats.

Transvaal was home to many still bitter over their recent defeat in the Boer War, and the colonial parliament split over whether to give the king the diamond. As a result, the king thought his dignity might require him to refuse it. A rising young politician named Winston Churchill, himself a veteran of the Boer War, convinced the king to accept the jewel.

Mine superintendent Frederick Wells received a $10,000 bonus for discovering the stone. Because one side of the diamond was smooth, experts believe it was only part of what was once a much larger diamond, broken up by natural forces.

THE MAN WHO SAVED FOOTBALL

Meet the father of football's forward pass: President Theodore Roosevelt.

I n October of 1905, President Theodore Roosevelt convened an urgent summit meeting at the White House. The subject: college football. The game had become so brutal that more than one hundred student players had died. College presidents were disbanding teams. Several state legislatures were giving serious consideration to making football illegal.

TR was himself a fan (his son played football at Harvard), but he had a harsh message for the men who ruled the game: Sooner or later the rising public outcry would force his hand. If they didn't change the rules to make football safer, he might have no choice but to ban it.

Roosevelt's call for reform prompted the formation of a new rules committee to make major changes to the game. One committee member suggested an idea long advocated by legendary coach John Heisman: legalizing the forward pass. That might open up the game, reducing dangerous mass collisions in the middle of the field.

The *New York Times* called the idea "radical," and the head of the rules committee was opposed to it. Nevertheless it was adopted for the 1906 season, along with rules that outlawed holding and unnecessary roughness and required a team to gain ten yards (instead of five) for a first down.

Though football purists decried the changes, they wound up making the game not only safer but also more popular than ever. Thanks to a play called by the president, football passed into a new era.

The New Game of **FOOTBALL**

Radical changes • • • • • in this year's rules revolutionize the sport

College football's first forward pass came on September 22, 1906, when Saint Louis University quarterback Brad Robinson heaved the ball to Jack Schneider in a game against Carroll College. (Robinson later became mayor of Saint Louis.) Saint Louis coach Eddie Cochems, an unsung pioneer of the passing game, was among the first to teach his players to throw the ball with their fingers on the laces to get a good spiral.

" **GET THE GAME PLAYED ON A THOROUGHLY CLEAN BASIS!** "

—PRESIDENT THEODORE
ROOSEVELT TO COLLEGE
FOOTBALL OFFICIALS

The new rules legalized the forward pass but heavily restricted its use. The ball could not be passed within five yards of the center, it could not be passed to a receiver in the end zone, and an incomplete pass automatically resulted in the other team getting the ball.

EIFFEL, OR EYESORE?

How a famous landmark was saved from certain destruction.

It is hard to imagine Paris without its most famous landmark, the Eiffel Tower. But when it was going up, there were many who thought it would be the ruin of the great city.

The famous tower was built for the Paris Centennial Exhibition in 1889. It was scheduled to stand for only twenty years—but for critics, that was twenty years too long. Construction was barely under way when a committee of fifty writers and artists launched a public campaign against what they called "the useless and monstrous Eiffel Tower." They bemoaned its "barbarous mass overwhelming and humiliating all our monuments." Other critics referred to the tower as a "a lamp post stuck in the belly of Paris" and "a giant ungainly skeleton."

The tower proved wildly popular among visitors, but many Parisians continued to regard it with a jaundiced eye. Its opponents kept up a drumbeat of criticism, and the government was determined that when the twenty years were up, the tower was coming down. Nothing, it seemed, could save it.

That is, until radio was invented, and proved to be the tower's salvation.

The thousand-foot structure turned out to be an excellent radio tower that could receive messages from far, far away. In 1907 the French government decided the tower could not come down—it was too valuable as an antenna. Function followed form this time around, and saved a Paris monument from certain destruction.

Within a year after commuting the tower's death sentence, the French government installed a state-of-the-art wireless facility capable of transmitting messages to the United States.

" **THIS STUPEFYING FOLLY…THIS ODIOUS COLUMN OF BOLTED METAL.** "

—ARTISTS' PROTEST AGAINST THE EIFFEL TOWER

Tourists never had any doubt about the tower. Two million visited when it opened in 1889, and millions more came during the Exposition of 1900, when this picture was taken.

AMERICA'S SPORT

The surprising origins of baseball: the facts and the myth.

The myth: baseball is a strictly American sport, invented by a Civil War hero, General Abner Doubleday. Where did that story come from? From a 1908 report sponsored by sporting goods millionaire A.G. Spalding. Determined to demonstrate that baseball was impeccably American, Spalding handpicked a committee of prominent people to examine the origins of the game. Then he spoon-fed them some pretty flimsy evidence suggesting that Doubleday not only designed but also named the sport back in 1839. The final report used that evidence to declare Doubleday the father of baseball.

But the report ignored a well-known British sport, rounders, which is also called by another name: baseball. Dating back to the mid-1700s, the game is played on a diamond-shaped field, and has a "feeder," who pitches the ball to a "striker," who is out if he misses three pitches. Sound familiar?

Abner Doubleday may never have even watched a baseball game. Still, he got the credit, because Spalding thought America needed its own game. Of course, it also made for good PR to help hype the sales of baseball equipment.

The reality: the origins of baseball are about as American as tea and crumpets.

Doubleday fired the first shot of the war for the Union, and later commanded troops at Gettysburg. But he was fourteen years in the grave before there was even a faint suggestion that he created baseball. The evidence: a single letter written by a man who claimed to be Doubleday's childhood friend in Cooperstown, New York.

Spalding's report had credibility because he was one of the most recognizable men in American sports. A star pitcher for Boston and Chicago who won forty-seven games one season, he later became manager and eventually owner of the Chicago team before going into the sporting goods business.

DOUBLE O POWELL

Come face-to-face with the inter-national man of mystery who founded the Boy Scouts.

The Boy Scout movement was launched by Robert (later Lord) Baden-Powell back in 1908. But the revered scout leader had another side. He was a spy for the British military, the James Bond of his day. He was so proud of his undercover exploits and his mastery of spy techniques that he detailed them in a book entitled *My Adventures As a Spy*.

He was a master of disguise, and developed many novel spy tactics, including the coded sketch—an innocent-looking drawing that contained hidden military secrets.

He spied for Britain on several different continents, barely escaping capture several times. Espionage was a game to him, and he pursued it with great zest. "Spying would be an intensely interesting sport, even if no great results were obtainable from it," he said. "For anyone who is tired of life, the life of a spy would be the very finest recuperation."

After his spying days were over, Baden-Powell went on to become a bonafide military hero. His defense of Mafeking in South Africa during the Boer War made him a national hero in Britain. It was after all this that he created the scouting movement.

66 **ROMANCE AND EXCITEMENT.** 99

—BADEN-POWELL, EXPLAINING
WHAT HE LOVED MOST
ABOUT SPYING

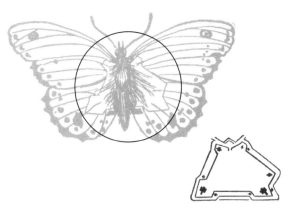

One of Baden-Powell's favorite tricks was to disguise himself as a naturalist (with trappings such as a butterfly net, sketchbook, and false beard) and then conceal diagrams of military installations inside what appeared to be innocent drawings of butterflies or grasshoppers.

WIRED WIRELESS

The aviation trailblazer whose legacy is music to our ears.

His name is not widely known today, but George Owen Squier was a true aviation pioneer. As a major in the Army Signal Corps, he supervised testing of the Wright Brothers' plane in 1908. His flight with Orville Wright made him one of the first passengers ever to ride in an airplane. Squier was instrumental in convincing the army to buy the Wright Flyer, thereby launching the age of military aviation. Later, during World War I, he rose to command of the Army Air Corps.

As if that wasn't enough, Squier was also a prolific inventor with more than sixty patents to his name. In 1911 he patented a technology that allowed many radio signals to travel over a single wire. He called it "wired wireless."

After Squier retired from the army, he launched a company to bring wired wireless to America. For $2 a month, consumers could have radio programs piped into their home over the electrical wires. It was an idea way ahead of its time—an early forerunner of cable TV. But people proved unwilling to pay for radio when they could get it for free. So Squier's company began targeting businesses, commissioning studies to show how piped-in music increased employee efficiency.

Squier's company was called Wired Radio, but in 1934 he came up with a catchier moniker, merging the word "music" with the name of his favorite hi-tech company, Kodak.

You may not know the name of George Owen Squier, but surely you know the name he gave his company: Muzak, now heard in stores, restaurants, malls, and offices by more than 100 million people a day.

S quier was lucky in the timing of his flight in the Wright Flyer. Thomas Selfridge, another army officer flying with Orville, was killed in a crash a few days later—becoming the first passenger ever to die in an airplane accident.

Squier's radio research led him in some strange directions. One subject of particular interest was tree telephony. He tried hammering copper nails into a tree to turn it into a radio antenna capable of receiving shortwave signals. He called this a "flora phone."

WRONG TURN TO WORLD WAR I

If one man had asked for directions, a war might never have begun.

June 28, 1914. Archduke Franz Ferdinand, heir to the Austro-Hungarian throne, visited one of the far-flung provinces of his empire, Bosnia. Then, as now, the area was seething with tension. Serbian revolutionaries conspired to kill the archduke while his motorcade drove through Sarajevo. One of the would-be assassins tossed a bomb at his car, but the archduke deftly batted it away. It exploded in the street, injuring one of his aides. "So you welcome your guests with bombs!" the indignant Ferdinand spluttered to local officials.

Later, the archduke insisted on visiting the injured aide in the hospital. Unfamiliar with the route, his driver took a wrong turn, and that made all the difference. An official shouted, "That's the wrong way," and the car stopped. Unfortunately, it did so right in front of one of the conspirators involved in the failed bombing. The surprised young man saw his opportunity, drew his Browning pistol and fired.

Within minutes Ferdinand and his wife were dead. The archduke's assassination triggered World War I, which would ultimately claim more than 10 million lives.

All because of one wrong turn.

After shooting the archduke, nineteen-year-old Gavrilo Princip tried to kill himself, but the cyanide pill he took turned out to be old and ineffective. Sentenced to life in prison, he died of consumption in 1918.

> ❝ **DO YOU THINK SARAJEVO IS FULL OF ASSASSINS?** ❞

—THE GOVERNOR OF BOSNIA, MAKING A CONDESCENDING REPLY TO A REQUEST FOR BODYGUARDS FROM THE ARCHDUKE'S AIDE

...phie tried to save her ...sband's life by throwing ...rself between him and the ...sassin. His last words ...re, "Don't die, Sophie, live ...r our children." But both ...ed of their wounds within ...inutes. It was their four-...enth wedding anniversary.

THE CABDRIVERS WHO SAVED PARIS

"Taxi...Take me to the front."

In August 1914, the Germans were driving relentlessly for Paris. They were less than forty miles away by the beginning of September. That's when French troops made a last-ditch stand at the river Marne. It seemed almost certain the French would be crushed, and their capital city captured.

There were six thousand soldiers in Paris that could help make the difference, but no way to get them to the front. Then one of the generals realized that if they could mobilize the taxicabs of Paris to carry the soldiers, they could do the job.

The word went out. Patriotic cabbies emptied out their passengers, explaining proudly that they had to "go to battle." Six hundred of them lined up at the

appointed hour. General Galliéni, military commander of Paris, came out to inspect them. *"Eh bien, voilà au moins qui n'est pas banal!"* he said. Roughly translated: "Here's something you don't see every day."

The soldiers were rushed to the front, and their presence helped stiffen resistance to the Germans. In what history has come to call the miracle of the Marne, the French army held firm. Paris was saved—thanks in part to the valor of her cabdrivers.

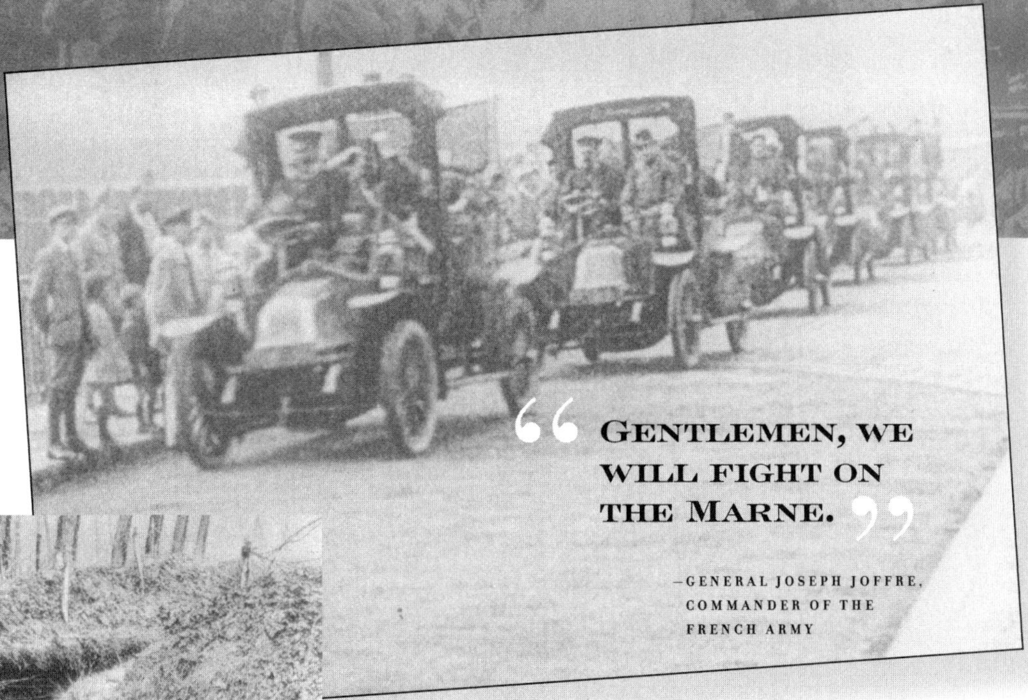

> ## GENTLEMEN, WE WILL FIGHT ON THE MARNE.

—GENERAL JOSEPH JOFFRE,
COMMANDER OF THE
FRENCH ARMY

The taxis, almost all of them Renaults, could each hold five men. Every taxi had to make the seventy-five-mile round trip to the front twice in order to bring up the soldiers.

The Battle of the Marne prevented Germany from winning a decisive victory at the outset of the war. It led, however, to four years of trench warfare that cost millions of lives.

STRIKE SONG

Please rise, and hear how the national anthem came to be played before ball games.

On September 11, 1918, game five of the World Series was scheduled for Fenway Park in Boston. The Red Sox were going to play the Chicago Cubs, and since this was during World War I, many wounded veterans would be in the stands.

The start of the game was delayed when a dispute arose over—guess what?—money. (There is, after all, nothing new in sports.) Players were upset that they weren't getting a bigger share of the World Series purse, so they decided to strike. They refused to take the field. Hasty negotiations took place under the stands as fans grew impatient.

After about an hour, the players reluctantly agreed to play ball for the sake of the vets. Caught up by the patriotic fervor (and no doubt trying to placate the restless crowd), the happy Red Sox owner had the band strike up "The Star-Spangled Banner." It was the first time the song is known to have been played before a ball game.

The wartime fans rose and doffed their hats out of respect, and a new tradition was born. The Red Sox went on to win the series, the last one they would capture in the twentieth century.

NATIONAL ANTHEM OPENS THE AFFRAY

Lively Battle Waged in Which Hippo Vaughn Is Controlling Factor Throughout.

BOSTON, Sept. 10.—The band played "The Star Spangled Banner" while the players and spectators stood with bared heads. Vaughn pitched for the Cubs, while Sam Jones, Boston's right-hander, was the selection for Boston.

The New York Times thought playing the anthem before the game so out of the ordinary that they devoted a headline to it. (It wasn't officially the national anthem yet, but it was already considered so by many people.)

> ## WE'LL PLAY...FOR THE SAKE OF THE WOUNDED SAILORS AND SOLDIERS WHO ARE IN THE GRANDSTANDS.

—HARRY HOOPER,
RED SOX OUTFIELDER

Red Sox outfielder Harry Hooper drew much criticism for his role in organizing the strike. A New York Times reporter sarcastically referred to him in print as "Comrade Hooper." A slightly hysterical Boston Post *columnist wrote: "Professional baseball is dead...killed by the greed of players and owners."*

FORGOTTEN FIGHT

The war with Russia
you never knew
we had.

American soldiers sent to Russia to fight the decisive war against communism. It sounds like a Tom Clancy fantasy, but it actually happened.

World War I was barely over when President Woodrow Wilson decided it was time for the United States to intervene in the Russian Civil War. He sent thousands of American troops to support the White Russians, who were trying to overthrow the new communist regime under Lenin. Britain, France, and Japan sent troops as well.

This was no cold war. The Allied Expeditionary Force fought a series of bloody engagements against the Bolsheviks in north Russia, losing hundreds of men. Another American division in Siberia also took casualties.

The halfhearted efforts proved too small to prevent a communist takeover, and the troops were pulled out by 1920. Quickly forgotten in the United States, the fighting was long remembered in the Soviet Union. It cemented Soviet distrust of the West, creating suspicions that eventually helped to fuel the Cold War.

In the bitter fighting outside of Archangel, in the far north, the main means of transportation was horse-drawn sleds. Here, Colonel George E. Stewart returns from a visit to the front.

U.S. troops march into the Siberian city of Vladivostok in August of 1918. In this forgotten war, the Japanese were our allies. An honor guard of Japanese marines stands at attention at the far left.

The military effort also had a propaganda component. The troops sent to Russia were accompanied by Signal Corps camera crews to bring back images of American boys going to war against communism.

CARBINE WILLIAMS

The prison inmate who helped outfit the U.S. Army.

In July of 1921, a sheriff's posse swooped down on a moonshiner's still in North Carolina. Shots rang out and a deputy was killed. Although he always swore that he never fired a shot, moonshiner David Marshall Williams was convicted of murder. Many called for the death penalty, but instead he was sentenced to thirty years hard labor.

In prison Williams secretly designed a gun. Working on a gun doesn't sound like the ideal activity for a prisoner, but when Williams showed the designs to Warden H.T. Peoples, the warden allowed him to go ahead and build the weapon. Peoples realized he was dealing with a mechanical genius who deserved to be encouraged. During his years in prison, Williams built six guns and invented the short-stroke piston, a device that captures the explosive force from the firing bullet and uses it to load the next one.

After eight years in prison Williams received a pardon from the governor. He started building weapons for the government and patenting his ideas. In 1941 Williams was working with Winchester when the army announced a competition for a new lightweight semiautomatic rifle. The winner was a model designed by Williams that featured his innovative short-stroke piston.

The new weapon was called the M1 carbine. It became the workhorse of World War II, appearing on soldiers' shoulders all over the world. Over 6 million were manufactured between 1940 and 1945, which made it the most-produced service weapon of the war.

Williams made his first gun when he was ten years old, carving it out of wood. He continued to make weapons in his North Carolina workshop until old age, and was granted more than sixty gun patents during his lifetime. He is seen here with a machine gun and an automatic weapon of his own design.

" ONE OF THE STRONGEST CONTRIBUTING FACTORS IN OUR VICTORY IN THE PACIFIC. "

—GENERAL DOUGLAS MACARTHUR
ON THE M1 CARBINE

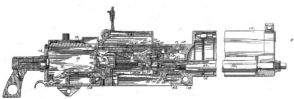

Williams (left) and a fellow inmate. When word got out about Williams's gun building, Warden Peoples found himself called on the carpet. He told the prison superintendent that he trusted Williams so much that if the prisoner ever used one of his guns in an escape, the warden would serve out the remainder of his time.

MAN'S BEST FRIEND

The medical emergency that helped inspire the world's most grueling race.

In January 1925, a deadly diphtheria epidemic broke out among the children of Nome, Alaska. The nearest lifesaving serum was in Anchorage, some seven hundred miles away. The snow-covered landscape was almost impassable, and a ship would take too long. To make matters worse, the only two airplanes in the state were in storage for the long winter.

The governor decided the serum would have to be "mushed" to Nome by a series of dogsled teams. Messages flew across telegraph lines to arrange the relay. The serum was rushed by rail to the town of Nenana. There it was handed to Wild Bill Shannon, whose dog team was the first of eighteen teams that would carry the serum 674 miles across the frozen tundra.

The conditions were frightening. The temperature dipped as low as forty below zero. Gale-force winds and blinding snow hampered the drivers. The whole world was riveted by their dramatic race against time and the elements; the progress of the sleds muscled other stories off front pages everywhere. On the fifth day, all contact with the sled carrying the serum was lost, and many feared the worst. But at five-thirty in the morning on February 1—127½ hours after the dogsled marathon began—Gunnar Kaassen emerged from the darkness to deliver the serum to Nome, led by his soon to be famous lead dog, Balto.

Today, the epic journey is commemorated annually in the great Anchorage-to-Nome dogsled race named after the trail on which much of it is run: the Iditarod.

Gunnar Kaassen's dog team arrived in Nome after traveling fifty-three miles. Balto (the black dog with the white front leg) quickly became a celebrity. He toured the country, and even had a statue erected in his honor in New York's Central Park. After his death his body was preserved and put on display at the Museum of Natural History in Cleveland.

> **I GAVE BALTO HIS HEAD AND TRUSTED HIM. HE NEVER FALTERED... THE CREDIT IS HIS.**
>
> —GUNNAR KAASSEN

Less famous than Balto but perhaps just as deserving of attention was another lead dog, Togo. Undefeated dogsled racer Leonhard Seppala drove Togo and his team nearly 150 miles just to get in position. Then they carried the serum ninety-one miles through a raging blizzard. To save time, Seppala took a dangerous shortcut across frozen Norton Bay, in conditions so awful he was forced to rely solely on Togo's sense of direction.

SCOPES TRIAL

One of the most famous trials of the century was actually a fraud.

When high school teacher John Scopes was put on trial in Dayton, Tennessee, for teaching evolution, the eyes of the entire nation were focused on the small town. Which, as it turns out, was exactly what the town fathers were hoping for when they cooked up the phony trial in the first place.

After Tennessee became one of three states to pass a law banning the teaching of evolution, the ACLU took out newspaper ads looking for a test case with which to challenge the law. The town fathers of Dayton saw this as an unprecedented opportunity for some self-promotion. They weren't trying to stop Scopes at all. He was in on the deal—they asked his permission before prosecuting him. Scopes wasn't even the regular biology teacher. He was a popular football coach who taught biology only as a substitute. Everyone agreed on the plan at Robinson's drugstore, where the prosecutors swore out a warrant that was handed to the accused.

As Scopes headed out to a tennis game, the prosecutor called the press with the news. Soon the entire nation was to be riveted by the controversial trial that was born as a PR ploy.

Famed defense attorney Clarence Darrow wasn't even trying to get Scopes acquitted. He wanted him convicted so that they could appeal the case to a higher court and generate more anticreationism publicity. In the end, Scopes was indeed convicted, but to the chagrin of his defense team, the judge let him off on a technicality.

> **HERE WAS AN UNEXAMPLED, ALMOST A MIRACULOUS CHANCE TO GET DAYTON UPON THE FRONT PAGES, TO MAKE IT TALKED ABOUT, TO PUT IT UPON THE MAP.**

—NEWSPAPERMAN H.L. MENCKEN

When the Dayton town fathers gathered in Robinson's drugstore, they wanted to make sure Scopes (seated, with glasses) had actually taught evolution. Scopes told them that virtually every single science teacher in the state did so. "Evolution is explained in Hunter's Civic Biology," he said, "and that's our textbook."

THE RACE TO END ALL RACES

The Olympic race that set back women's sports for more than thirty years.

The crowd was cheering wildly as the runners rounded the final curve in the women's 800 meters at the 1928 Olympic Games. This was the first year women were allowed to run such a long distance, and it was an exciting race. In the final moments, Germany's Lina Radke pulled ahead to win gold and set a new world record that would stand for more than a decade.

After the race, several women fell to the ground in exhaustion, and some had to be given aid. That sort of thing happened all the time to male athletes. But critics pounced on this as proof that women shouldn't be running at all. The *London Daily Mail* quoted a doctor who said that such "feats of endurance" could make women "old too soon." The president of the International Olympic Committee called for eliminating all women's sports from the Olympics and returning to the custom of the ancient Greeks, who allowed only men to compete.

It sounds silly to our modern ears, but the results were anything but. Women were banned from Olympic races longer than 200 meters for thirty-two years. It was 1960 before female Olympians could again compete in longer events, their race for equality slowed to a crawl... by ignorance.

> “WOMEN...ARE NOT PHYSICALLY BUILT TO UNDERGO THE STRAIN THAT MEN ARE CAPABLE OF.”

—ANONYMOUS DOCTOR QUOTED IN THE *LONDON DAILY MAIL*, AUGUST 1928

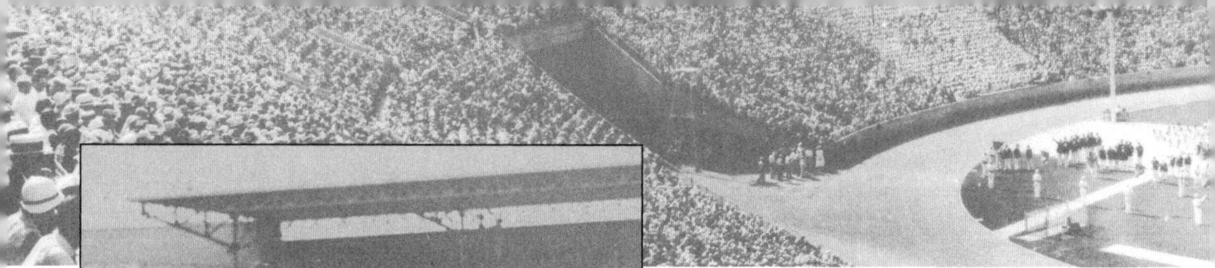

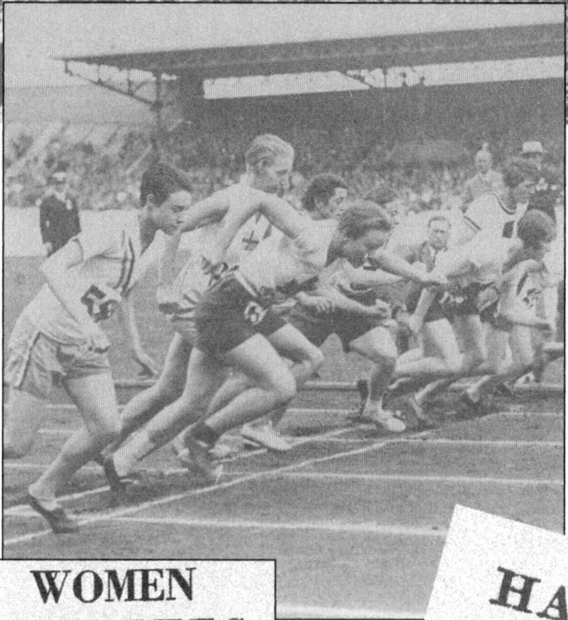

WOMEN ATHLETES COLLAPSE.

FIERCE STRAIN OF OLYMPIC RACE.

SOBBING GIRLS.

FROM SIR PERCIVAL PHILLIPS.

HARMFUL FEATS.

DOCTOR CONDEMNS RACES FOR WOMEN.

Dr. S. Hemming Belfrage, honorary secretary of the New Health Society, said to a *Daily Mail* reporter last night:

There is not the slightest doubt that these strenuous and unnecessary feats of endurance on the part of women are harmful to the individuals and to the race generally.

I have strongly urged that wo... should take up healthy ga... do much to improve ... nation, but th... are bot...

THE MOLD THAT SAVED MILLIONS

How did a messy research lab lead to the development of a wonder drug?

There was nothing unusual about the fact that Scottish biologist Alexander Fleming failed to clean up his lab before going on holiday in the summer of 1928. Friends often teased Fleming for being disorderly. The truth is that he was very hesitant to throw out his old bacteria cultures until absolutely sure that there was nothing more to learn from them.

He came back from vacation to find some petri dishes had grown moldy. Sorting through them prior to throwing them out, he discovered that the mold in one dish had destroyed the bacteria culture he was growing there. The mold was a kind of fungus, penicillium, that grows on bread. Fleming wrote a scientific paper on his discovery, but never really followed up on its practical applications.

During World War II, a team of scientists searching for a way to treat infected wounds came across Fleming's discovery and began to experiment with a form of the mold. Its powers proved almost miraculous. Soon it was being manufactured in unbelievable quantities and rushed to the front.

More than fifty years later, penicillin remains the world's most used antibiotic. Thanks to a scientist who didn't like to clean up.

More than twenty-one chemical companies participated in a crash program to manufacture lifesaving penicillin during World War II. By war's end they were manufacturing 650 billion units per month.

THAT'S FUNNY...

—FLEMING, HIS VOICE TRAILING
OFF, WHEN HE DISCOVERED
THE MOLDY DISH

Fleming shared in a Nobel Prize for his serendipitous discovery, about which he dryly commented: "One sometimes finds what one is not looking for."

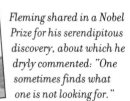

GUNFIGHTER GOLDEN YEARS

The unlikely final days of two real-life Western heroes.

Wyatt Earp and Bat Masterson: legendary lawmen of the Old West. Masterson, the mild-mannered Dodge City sheriff, was said to have killed twenty-six men before he turned thirty. Earp, his onetime deputy, achieved undying fame after the gunfight at the OK Corral. They walked tall, shot fast, and each earned himself a reputation that soon became enshrined in myth and legend.

And then they rode off into the sunset, right? Truth is, both men outlived the Wild West by many years.

After years in Alaska, Wyatt Earp headed to Hollywood and spent his last days in showbiz. He became great friends with early Western star William Hart and spent hours teaching him how to quick-draw before dying in 1929.

Bat Masterson went back east and settled down in New York City. He lived until 1921, ending his multifaceted career as a sports columnist for the *New York Telegraph*, where he died at his desk…with his boots on.

In this photograph of the Dodge City Peace Commission, Wyatt Earp is second from the left in the front row and Bat Masterson is at the far right in the back. The picture was taken in 1883, two years after the gunfight at the OK Corral.

One of the people whom Wyatt Earp
befriended in Hollywood was a young
propman named Marion Morrison,
who as an actor took the name
John Wayne. Wayne later said he
based his portrayal of Western
lawmen on his conversations
with Earp.

In later years Masterson became good friends
with President Theodore Roosevelt and visited him numerous times in the White
House.

THE SEARCH FOR PLANET X

Meet the farmhand who helped map the solar system.

In 1928, Clyde Tombaugh was working on his father's farm in Kansas. In love with the night sky, he built a telescope using parts from a cream separator and his dad's 1910 Buick. He made drawings of the planets and sent them to the Lowell Observatory in Arizona. Even though he had only a high school diploma, the observatory offered him a job.

There he was put to work searching for a planet that might not even exist. The founder of the observatory, Percival Lowell, had spent years searching for an unseen Planet X that he believed was affecting the orbit of Neptune. After he died, he left money for the search to continue. Many astronomers were skeptical. "If there were any more planets to be found," said one, "they would have been found by now."

Tombaugh had to photograph the sky quadrant by quadrant, then compare the photographs two at a time, in search of movement that might suggest a planet. Thousands of photographs, each containing thousands of stars. It was grinding work.

On February 18, 1930, he saw a dim speck move slightly as he switched between two photographs. The farm boy from Kansas became the first American to discover a planet…which was named Pluto.

Percival Lowell was proved right in his belief that there was another planet out there. He was somewhat less correct in his famous contention that the canals he thought he observed on Mars were proof that it was inhabited by a race of intelligent beings.

Tombaugh went on to get a Ph.D. and work for the space program. When he was in his eighties, the Smithsonian asked him if it could have his original telescope. Tombaugh's answer: "I told them I was still using it."

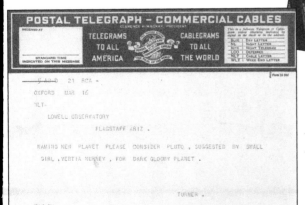

All over the world, people suggested names for the new planet. An eleven-year-old girl in Oxford, England, named Venetia Burney (misspelled in this telegram) proposed Pluto, after the mythological god of the underworld. The name had another thing going for it...the first two letters are the initials of Percival Lowell.

GOING...GOING...GONE

The best home run hitter of all time— barred from the big leagues?

He was called the black Babe Ruth. But there are those who say Ruth should be known as the white Josh Gibson. In the '30s and '40s, this powerful catcher was one of the greatest stars of the Negro Leagues. And he may well have been the greatest home run hitter of all time.

Records are sketchy, but Gibson is credited with a total of more than 800 home runs in his seventeen-year career, hitting 89 in one season and 75 in another. He could also hit for average—he led the Negro Leagues in batting four times.

Gibson hit the ball so hard he is said to have broken the backs of numerous wooden seats in the outfield grandstands. The *New York Daily News* wrote that any team in baseball would benefit from signing him. "He hit the ball a mile," mused Hall of Fame pitcher Walter Johnson. "Too bad Gibson is a colored fellow."

The tragedy of his life was that Gibson never played a day in the majors, because during his career blacks were kept out. Several major league teams came close to making the plunge and signing Gibson, but none ever did. His friends believed that it broke his heart. He died of a massive stroke when he was only thirty-five—just a few months before Jackie Robinson broke baseball's color line forever.

According to the Sporting News, Josh Gibson swatted the longest home run ever hit in Yankee Stadium—a monster ball that went 580 feet, longer than anything that Babe Ruth, Hank Aaron, or anyone else ever hit.

" THE ONLY WAY TO PITCH TO HIM WAS TO PITCH BEHIND HIM. "

—CHET BREWER, NEGRO LEAGUE PITCHER

JOSHUA (JOSH) GIBSON
NEGRO LEAGUES 1930-1946
CONSIDERED GREATEST SLUGGER IN NEGRO
BASEBALL LEAGUES. POWER-HITTING CATCHER
WHO HIT ALMOST 800 HOME RUNS IN LEAGUE
AND INDEPENDENT BASEBALL DURING HIS
17-YEAR CAREER. CREDITED WITH HAVING
BEEN NEGRO NATIONAL LEAGUE BATTING
CHAMPION IN 1936-38-42-45.

Gibson is one of a handful of players who made it into the Baseball Hall of Fame without ever playing an inning of major league baseball. Most of those are veterans of the Negro Leagues.

DON'T MESS WITH THANKSGIVING!

A lesson one president had to learn the hard way.

In 1939, Thanksgiving was scheduled to fall on the last day of November. Retailers lobbied President Franklin Roosevelt to move it one week earlier in order to lengthen the Christmas shopping season.

FDR wanted to do anything he could to help a still shaky economy, so he agreed. In the middle of August he casually announced to reporters that Thanksgiving would come a week early that year, and the next as well.

The decision quickly became front-page news, and it sparked a firestorm of controversy. The White House was flooded with letters, and cartoonists had a field day. Especially aggrieved were calendar makers—whose products were suddenly inaccurate—and high school football coaches, upset to find that the big Thanksgiving game was no longer on the right day.

The issue divided the country. Twenty-three states decide to celebrate on the original date, while twenty-three others went along with the new date

proclaimed by Roosevelt. Texas and Colorado, unable to decide, celebrated both.

The following year Roosevelt sheepishly admitted that the whole thing was a mistake and returned Thanksgiving to its original date. Congress passed a law setting that date in stone, so that no president could ever again mess with Thanksgiving.

MOVING UP THE GOAL POSTS

> ## THE PROTESTANTS
> ## WILL RAISE HELL.

—ROOSEVELT AIDE STEVE EARLY, IN A
MEMO TO THE PRESIDENT ON CHANGING
THANKSGIVING

*Many letter writers mocked
what they saw as a perfect
example of FDR's high-
handedness. Others who
complained to the presi-
dent included couples
with Thanksgiving
wedding plans and
children with Thanks-
giving birthdays.*

*resident Roosevelt
eriously considered moving
hanksgiving to a Monday,
 give workers a three-day
veekend, but reluctantly
ropped the idea when
ides convinced him
hat religious leaders
vouldn't go for it.*

Was   . C.

Mr. President:

I see by the paper this morning where you
want to change Thanksgiving Day to
November 23 of.which I heartily approve.
Thanks.

Now, there are some things that I would
like done and would appreciate your
approval:

1. Have Sunday changed to
   Wednesday;

2. Have Monday's to be
   Christmas;

3. Have it strictly against
   the Will of God to work
   on Tuesday;

4. Have Thursday to be Pay
   Day with time and one-half
   for overtime;

5. Require everyone to take
        ay and Saturday off
           trip down

EINSTEIN'S ERROR

*What Albert
Einstein considered
his greatest mistake.*

Have you ever written a letter and wished you could take it back? Albert Einstein wrote a letter like that in 1939. Concerned by reports that German scientists had succeeded in splitting the atom, Einstein wrote to FDR suggesting that recent nuclear research might make it possible to build "extremely powerful bombs of a new type." Einstein advised speeding up research—before the Germans got there first. He also recommended that the United States take action to secure an adequate supply of uranium.

This letter set off a chain reaction of its own, eventually resulting in the Manhattan Project—the enormous effort to create the first atomic bomb.

By 1945, many scientists were alarmed by the power of this new weapon—especially since it was now clear that Germany wasn't building one of its own. Einstein wrote FDR another letter, asking him to meet with scientists who opposed its use. But the president died before he could read it.

Einstein later said the first letter was "the single greatest mistake" of his entire life.

The Manhattan Project eventually involved tens of thousands of people, of whom only a handful knew what they were trying to accomplish. The result: a bomb ten feet long with a yield equivalent to twenty thousand tons of high explosives. This is Fat Boy, the bomb dropped on Nagasaki.

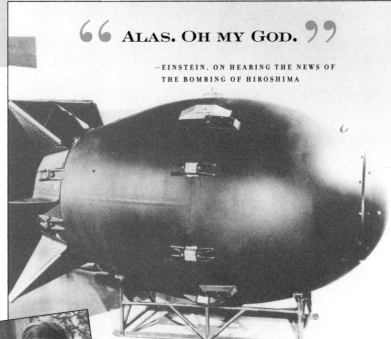

66 ALAS. OH MY GOD. 99

—EINSTEIN, ON HEARING THE NEWS OF
THE BOMBING OF HIROSHIMA

Einstein wrote both letters to Roosevelt at the urging of Dr. Leo Szilard, a brilliant Hungarian physicist who worked on the Manhattan Project. In happier times, the two scientists also patented a refrigerator, which they sold to Electrolux.

JAPAN'S SCHINDLER

How did an obscure Japanese diplomat save thousands from the Holocaust?

When Hitler's blitzkrieg exploded into Poland in 1939, thousands of Polish Jews fled to neighboring Lithuania. But it was only a temporary refuge. By the summer of 1940, with the Soviet Union now occupying Lithuania and the Nazis on the march, danger was closing in.

The dilemma the refugees faced was that they needed travel documents to get out—and no government was prepared to issue them. A sympathetic Dutch diplomat hatched an unlikely plan to get them out via the Soviet Union and Japan. But his scheme hinged on refugees being able to get hard-to-obtain Japanese transit visas—and fast. Without those visas the refugees would be trapped.

At this dark hour, a surprising savior appeared: Chiune Sugihara, the Japanese consul general in Kaunas, Lithuania. Against the orders of his government, he began to issue precious travel visas to desperate refugees. Sugihara granted visas to any who applied, whether they had the right documents or not. He issued thousands of visas even as his superiors kept ordering him not to. Finally, Tokyo ordered him to leave, but even at the train station he continued to hand lifesaving visas out the window of the train.

Ultimately, Sugihara's efforts saved at least five thousand Jews from the Holocaust—and cost him his job with the Japanese Foreign Ministry. Why did Sugihara defy his government and destroy his career? "They were human beings, and they needed help," he said. "I'm glad I found the strength to give it to them."

> ## 66 EVEN A HUNTER CANNOT KILL A BIRD WHICH FLIES TO HIM FOR REFUGE. 99

—SAMURAI MAXIM OFTEN
QUOTED BY CHIUNE SUGIHARA

*One of those saved by Sugihara was Susan Bluman.
She and her newlywed husband were missing papers
normally required for a transit visa, and she didn't
even have a valid passport—just her picture pasted in
her husband's passport. Sugihara simply ignored the
rules and gave them a visa.*

LIVE AND LET SPY

Reality and fiction come together in the world of espionage.

William Donovan is famous as the founder of the OSS, the World War II spy agency that was the forerunner of the CIA. When Donovan was setting up the agency, he consulted with a trusted friend, a British naval officer who was the assistant to the head of British Naval Intelligence.

The officer was eager to help Donovan. Furthermore, he was a man of great imagination, with a keen eye for detail. He stayed in a spare bedroom at Donovan's house in Washington, D.C., and drafted several detailed memos advising Donovan how to organize an American intelligence agency. Donovan went to work, and the rest is history.

The British officer was Commander Ian Lancaster Fleming. After the war he moved to Jamaica, where he drew upon his wartime experiences (and fantasies) to write a series of novels about an espionage agent who knew no equal, and who, like Fleming himself, was a bit of a lady's man. So it is that the man who had a hand in creating the CIA also created the world's most famous *fictional* spy.

The name is Bond. James Bond.

Donovan clearly valued Fleming's contributions. He presented Fleming with a .38 caliber police revolver, engraved with the words "For Special Services." It became one of his prized possessions.

Sean Connery was the quintessential Bond on screen. Fleming gave the Bond character many of his distinctive tastes: vodka martinis, for instance, shaken, not stirred. Fleming's secret designation in Navy Intelligence was Agent 17-F. Bond, of course, was 007.

When Fleming saw a bird-watching book written by an ornithologist named James Bond, he knew it was the perfect name for his spy: "brief, unromantic, yet very masculine." Later, when the ornithologist's wife, Mary, jokingly threatened to sue Fleming, he wrote back: "I can only offer your James Bond unlimited use of the name Ian Fleming for any purpose he may think fit."

BEAUTIFUL BRAINS

She pioneered on-screen nudity... and helped revolutionize communications.

Hedy Lamarr was just a teenager when she shocked the world in 1933 by appearing nude in the Czech film *Extase* (in English, *Ecstasy*). It was the movie industry's first nude scene.

When Hedy hit Hollywood, she was billed as "the most beautiful woman in the world." But after World War II broke out, she was determined to put her brains to work for her adopted country.

In August 1942, Lamar got together with composer George Antheil and patented a secret communications system to prevent the jamming of radio-controlled torpedoes. At its heart was an innovation Hedy dreamed up on the back of a cocktail napkin: frequency hopping. In other words, radio signals that constantly switched frequencies to make interception impossible.

It was way ahead of its time, and wasn't put to use until the Cuban missile crisis, twenty years later. Today it has a fancier name—spread spectrum technology—and is a critical part of cell phone systems, satellite encryption, and other modern marvels.

A testament to the actress who was "heady" in every sense of the word.

ince her patent expired before it was used, Hedy never made a
ime off her idea. But she did eventually receive recognition.
he died on January 19, 2000, remembered for her beauty and
er brains.

> ## ❝ ANY GIRL CAN BE GLAMOROUS. ALL YOU HAVE TO DO IS STAND STILL AND LOOK STUPID. ❞
>
> —HEDY LAMARR

n Ecstasy's famous nude
cene, Hedy is skinny-dipping
vhen she discovers her horse
as run off. She goes trotting
fter him, au naturel, until
he comes face-to-face with
strange man in the woods.
ame by today's standards—
s most risqué shot is a glimpse
f Hedy's breasts—the sequence
ed to the film being condemned
y the pope and banned in
he United States.

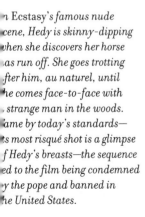

After making Ecstasy, *Hedy married
Austrian arms dealer Fritz Mandel. It was
from him that she received an education
in weapons and warfare. He was a Nazi
sympathizer who held his young bride a
virtual prisoner. She escaped by drugging
the maid and climbing out a second-
story window. After that she fled Europe
and came to the United States.*

THE DEAD MAN WHO DUPED HITLER

The contribution of a corpse that helped win the battle before it started.

I n early 1943 the Allies were getting ready to invade Nazi-occupied Europe from north Africa. Their destination was the island of Sicily. For the invasion to succeed, it was absolutely critical that the enemy be caught off guard. So British officers concocted a fantastic scheme.

Code name: Operation Mincemeat.

They grabbed a corpse from a London morgue and gave him a completely new identity. He was outfitted with a uniform, and papers placed in his pockets identified him as Major William Martin, a military courier. A briefcase was chained to his wrist. Inside, British spymasters planted forged documents suggesting that the target of the invasion would be Greece, not Sicily. Then a British submarine dropped the body of "Major Martin" off the coast of Spain, making it look as if he was a military courier who died in a plane crash.

As hoped, Spanish authorities showed the papers to the Germans. They were completely fooled. The news was rushed to Hitler, who made the defense of Greece his top priority. The German High Command sent Panzer units there, and Hitler ordered the famed General Erwin Rommel to Athens to mastermind the battle.

But there would be no battle in Greece. Instead, forces under Generals Bernard Montgomery and George Patton came ashore in Sicily, where German forces were ill prepared for them. Victory was made possible with the help of the man who never was.

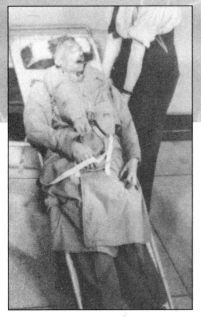

For more than fifty years after the war, the identity of the body remained a closely held secret by the British government. In 1995 it was revealed that he was a thirty-four-year-old homeless man named Glyndwr Michael, who committed suicide by eating rat poison.

"MINCEMEAT SWALLOWED WHOLE"

—MESSAGE TO WINSTON CHURCHILL ANNOUNCING SUCCESS OF THE MISSION

Great care was taken in placing just the right items on the body to create a convincing illusion of a real person. Love letters, overdue bills, an old bus ticket, and various personal items all helped convince the Germans that Major Martin was genuine.

CLOSE CALL OF THE PORTER

The friendly fire that almost changed the course of World War II.

On November 14, 1943, President Roosevelt and the country's top military brass were secretly crossing the Atlantic aboard the USS *Iowa* on their way to an Allied summit meeting in Tehran. Tremendous care was taken to hide the identity of the VIPs in order to assure their safety. But suddenly a torpedo was seen heading straight for them.

How could the Germans have known?

They didn't. The escort ship USS *William D. Porter* had accidentally fired the torpedo during a drill. As danger alarms went off and crewmen headed to battle stations, the battleship *Iowa* maneuvered sharply and avoided the torpedo, which exploded just one hundred yards off the stern. The force of the explosion rocked the *Iowa* so violently that one officer aboard shouted, "My God, he hit us!" But the ship was not harmed at all.

History records a successful summit that helped secure an Allied victory. But there could have been a very different outcome—if not for a near miss.

Roosevelt was on his way to a summit with Stalin and Churchill. When the torpedo warning came over the loudspeaker, Roosevelt told his valet: "Take me over to the starboard side, I want to watch the torpedo."

After the incident, the USS Porter was escorted to Bermuda, where the entire crew was placed under arrest. "You never saw so many people coming and going, interrogations all night long," says former crewman Bob Jones. The captain was transferred to a desk job, and the Porter was ordered to the Aleutian Islands. It is said that after that, other ships often hailed her with the greeting "Don't shoot—we're Republicans!"

" TORPEDO! TORPEDO ON THE STARBOARD BEAM! "

—LOUDSPEAKER WARNING ON THE USS *IOWA*

A year later the Porter was hit by a kamikaze off Okinawa and became the only destroyer in the war to sink without the loss of a single man. Nearby ships were able to pluck all the survivors out of the water.

THE LITTLE BOAT THAT WON THE WAR

He was only a businessman, but Ike called him "the man who won the war for us."

D-Day. June 1944. More than 150,000 soldiers stormed the beaches of Normandy. They made it ashore successfully due in large part to one man: Andrew Jackson Higgins.

This hot-tempered New Orleans boatbuilder specialized in shallow draft boats perfect for prospectors and trappers in the Louisiana swamps. He was convinced he could build better landing craft than the Navy, and determined to prove it. Navy experts didn't think much of Higgins, though, or his crazy notion that landing craft should be built out of wood.

Higgins launched a one-man crusade to get the Navy brass to admit his boats were better. He browbeat admirals and built prototypes with his own money. He once gave a tongue-lashing to a roomful of high-ranking officers, shouting that "the Navy doesn't know a goddamn thing about small boats. But I do, by God." Finally, when Senator Harry Truman forced a head-to-head competition, Higgins beat the Navy boat hands down.

But that's only half the story. Higgins also turned out to be a mass-production genius, manufacturing more than twenty thousand landing craft and torpedo boats over the course of the war. More GIs hit the beaches in Higgins's boats than in all other landing craft combined. Without them, said General Eisenhower, D-Day might never have been possible.

The tough-talking Higgins became a wartime celebrity. His complaints about red tape became widely known as "bellows from the bayou." Even Hitler took notice, calling Higgins "the American Noah."

THE GUY WHO RELAXES IS HELPING THE AXIS!

In 1939, Higgins had less than a hundred employees. By 1944 he had more than twenty-five thousand people working at eight plants. When he ran out of room in one factory, he closed off a city street and started a production line right there. Desperate on another occasion for raw materials, he stole them from an oil refinery in Texas. "This man certainly is a wonder," said the Commandant of the Marines.

" WHERE THE
HELL WOULD
THE AMPHIBIOUS
FORCES HAVE
BEEN WITHOUT
YOU AND YOUR
BOATS? "

—MARINE GENERAL HOLLAND
SMITH, IN A LETTER TO HIGGINS

LOST IN TRANSLATION

A single word that may have made all the difference.

By July 1945, the war-weary Japanese government was ready to surrender. When the cabinet first received unofficial word of the surrender terms laid out by the Allied leaders meeting in Potsdam, they considered the terms lenient and were inclined to accept. But they decided to withhold comment until they receive the Allied ultimatums through official channels.

With that in mind, elderly premier Kantaro Suzuki tried to tread a careful path when questioned about the Potsdam Declaration. Unfortunately, he used a word that has two meanings. He told a press conference that the cabinet was adopting a position of *mokusatsu.*

The word *mokusatsu* can mean "withhold comment for the moment." It can also mean "ignore." The Japanese News Agency mistakenly translated it the second way. Radio Tokyo flashed the mistake to the world. Headlines in the United States blared that Japan was ignoring the declaration, rejecting the surrender terms.

The results were nothing short of tragic. President Truman decided that he had no choice but to go ahead and drop the atomic bomb. More than a hundred thousand people were killed and the cities of Hiroshima and Nagasaki virtually destroyed—in part because one old man chose the wrong word.

Just three days after reports that the Japanese were ignoring surrender terms, Harry Truman scribbled this note giving the go-ahead for dropping the bomb.

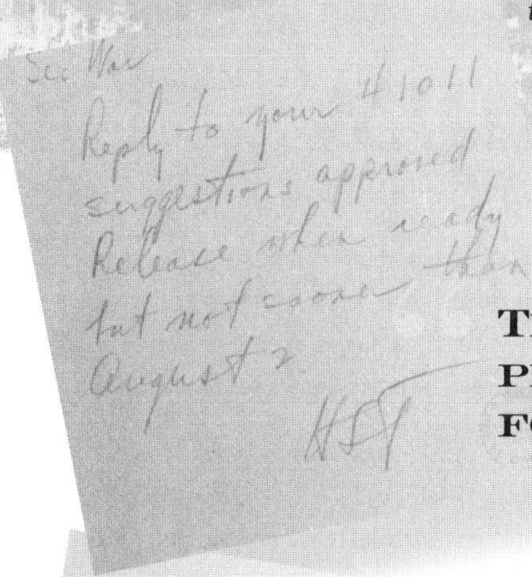

Sec War

Reply to your #1011
suggestions approved
Release when ready
but not sooner than
August 2

HST

THIS WAS A PIECE OF FOOLHARDINESS. 99

—TOSHIKAZU KASE,
JAPANESE FOREIGN OFFICE

Mokusatsu is made up of two characters: *moku*, meaning "silence," and *satsu* meaning "kill." Thus the literal translation, "to kill with silence."

The first atomic bomb was dropped on Hiroshima on August 6, 1945. This fire station was nearly a mile from ground zero.

1945

COOKING WITH RADAR

A kitchen essential that was essentially an accident.

In the summer of 1945, engineer Percy Spencer was conducting tests on a magnetron. That's the powerful tube at the heart of every radar set. When he reached into his pocket for a chocolate bar, he found instead a gooey mess. He wondered if the magnetron could be responsible.

Spencer was an engineering genius who had already helped win World War II by devising an improved magnetron tube that was easy to mass-produce, making possible the manufacture of tens of thousands of radar sets. Now he was ready to make his contribution to postwar America. Curious to see just what was going on, he put a bag of corn kernels in front of the magnetron. *Voilà!* The first-ever batch of microwave popcorn.

Spencer patented the new method of cooking. His employer, the Raytheon Company, transformed his discovery into the Radarange. The earliest model weighed 750 pounds and had a price tag of $3,000. Sales were limited. It took more than twenty years for this big daddy of all microwaves to spawn the new generation that today graces kitchens everywhere.

Percy Spencer never had more than a third-grade education, but this self-taught engineering legend wound up with more than 150 patents.

" WHO'S GOING TO PAY $500 FOR A HOT DOG WARMER? "

–EXPERTS CLAIMING
THE MICROWAVE
WOULD NEVER SELL

Raytheon's first Radarange was so big and expensive it made sense only in places like hotel kitchens and railroad dining cars. Today nine out of ten American homes have a microwave—albeit, a good deal smaller than the original.

ABOUT-FACE

*Imagine saving
the life of an ally
who winds up
becoming your most
bitter foe.*

In 1945 an American intelligence team code-named Deer parachuted into the jungles of Asia to help a band of guerrillas fighting the Japanese. They found the leader of the guerrillas, Nguyen Ai Quoc, seriously ill from malaria and dysentery. "This man doesn't have long for this world," exclaimed the team medic, but he successfully nursed him back to health. The grateful leader agreed to provide intelligence and rescue downed American pilots in return for ammunition and weapons.

The team suggested that the United States continue to support Quoc after the war, but the recommendation was considered too controversial and it was ignored. The following year the guerrilla leader pleaded with President Truman to support his movement to gain independence from the French, but the U.S. government decided it didn't like his politics.

Nguyen Ai Quoc was also known by another name: "He who enlightens." In Vietnamese: Ho Chi Minh. Sixty thousand Americans died in the Vietnam War, battling a former ally whose life the United States once fought to save.

*In the 1920s Ho worked as a busboy at
the Parker House Hotel in Boston.
By 1954 he had become president of an
independent North Vietnam. By the
1960s, the onetime U.S. ally was
America's public enemy number one.*

Ho Chi Minh (second from right) *with members of the OSS Deer team that saved his life. In the white suit at left is Vo Nguyen Giap, who later became Ho's military commander and masterminded military efforts against France and the United States.*

HANOI FEBRUARY 28 1946

MAR

VIỆT-NAM DÂN CHỦ CỘNG HÒA

CHÍNH PHỦ LÂM THỜI

BO NGOAI GIAO

*

TELEGRAM

PRESIDENT HOCHIMINH VIETNAM DEMOCRATIC REPUBLIC HANOI

TO THE PRESIDENT OF THE UNITED STATES OF AMERICA WASHINGTON D.C.

ON BEHALF OF VIETNAM GOVERNMENT AND PEOPLE I BEG TO INFORM YOU

THAT IN COURSE OF CONVERSATIONS BETWEEN VIETNAM GOVERNMENT AND FRENCH

REPRESENTATIVES THE LATTER REQUIRE THE SECESSION OF COCHINCHINA AND T

RETURN OF FRENCH TROOPS IN HANOI STOP MEANWHILE FRENCH POPULATION AND

TROOPS ARE MAKING ACTIVE PREPARATIONS FOR A COUP DE MAIN IN HANOI AND

FOR MILLTARY AGGRESSION STOP I THEREFORE MOST EARNESTLY APPEAL TO YOU

PERSONALLY AND TO THE AMERICAN PEOPLE TO INTERFERE URGENTLY IN SUPPORT

OF OUR INDEPENDENCE AND HELP MAKING THE NEGOTIATIONS MORE IN KEEPING W

THE PRINCIPLES OF THE ATLANTIC AND SAN FRANCISCO CHARTERS

HOCHIMINH

AMERICAN PIE

*What do UFOs
and good old
American pie have
in common?*

In the summer of 1947, the United States went UFO crazy. After an object that many believed to be a flying saucer crashed near Roswell, New Mexico, there was a frenzy of sightings of unidentified flying objects around the country.

California inventor Walter Frederick Morrison, hoping to cash in on America's sudden UFO obsession, created a toy that flew like a saucer. He and a partner started selling these Flyin' Saucers in California, but sales were hardly out of this world.

Morrison went back to the drawing board and devised a vastly improved model that he named the Pluto Platter. It became a big hit with California college kids, which is how it came to the attention of the brand new Wham-O toy company.

In 1957 Wham-O started distributing Pluto Platters across the country, promoting them heavily on college campuses. When one of the Wham-O founders visited Yale University, he found students there had been playing a lawn game for over thirty years in which they tossed around metal pie tins. Just as golfers shout "Fore," the students throwing the pie tins shouted out the name of the pie company emblazoned on them: "Frisbie!"

Wham-O, already wondering if "Pluto" was passé, adopted the name Frisbee (altering the spelling in the process) and a national craze was launched.

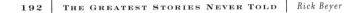

Walter Frederick Morrison would
do almost anything to market
his Pluto Platters. He was
selling them out of his trunk on
a street corner when the young
founders of Wham-O—
Rich Knerr and A. K. Melin—
first approached him to buy
the rights to the product.

In its prime, the Frisbie Pie
Company boasted a fleet of two
hundred trucks that delivered
eighty thousand pies a day.
Workers in the Bridgeport,
Connecticut, pie factory who
threw around the pie tins on
lunch break were arguably the
world's first Frisbee aficionados.

ONE OF THE FLEET OF 200 TRUCKS, FRISBIE PIE CO., BRIDGEPORT AND HARTFORD, CONN.

A DOG'S LIFE

*Meet the space
pioneer who was
nothing to bark at.*

In October of 1957, Americans were amazed to discover that the Soviet Union had put up the world's first satellite: Sputnik. The 184-pound satellite orbited the earth every ninety minutes, its signature beeping easily heard on radio sets around the globe.

Less than a month later, the Soviets did it again. They put up a much bigger satellite, with the world's first orbital space traveler: Laika, a mutt picked up from the streets. Moscow radio announced that Laika was riding in air-conditioned comfort as she rocketed through space at eighteen thousand miles an hour.

Unfortunately, the Russians did not yet have the technology to bring Laika back. Her oxygen ran out after a few days, and eventually her satellite burned up after its orbit decayed and it reentered the earth's atmosphere.

Although she never got home, Laika proved beyond all doubt that space travel was possible. And the two satellites rocketed into space by the Russians shocked the worried United States into launching its own space program.

The space race was on—thanks, in part, to the dog nicknamed Muttnick.

One of America's first astro-animals was a chimpanzee named Ham. He rode a Mercury capsule on a suborbital trip in 1961 that paved the way for his human follow-up act, Al Shepherd. Another chimp, named Enos, was the first American in orbit.

The first space travelers to make it back alive were a pair of Russian dogs named Belka and Strelka, who went up on August 19, 1960, and were successfully recovered after a day in orbit. Strelka eventually gave birth to puppies, one of which was given to American president John F. Kennedy. When that dog had puppies, JFK called them "pupniks."

A PIECE OF TAPE

The piece of masking tape that toppled a president.

Security guard Frank Wills was making his nightly rounds when he found a piece of tape covering a latch on a basement door. He assumed some worker in the office complex had left it there to make it easier to get in and out. Shaking his head, he removed it.

An hour or so later, he found the latch retaped. This time he called the police. They locked all the doors, shut off the elevators, and started searching the building. When they reached the sixth floor, they caught five burglars hiding behind desks in one of the offices.

Pretty routine case, except that the burglars were bugging the offices of the Democratic National Committee at the Washington, D.C., Watergate complex. Two reporters, Robert Woodward and Carl Bernstein, tirelessly pursued the story. The ensuing Watergate scandal consumed the presidency of Richard Nixon and eventually forced his resignation.

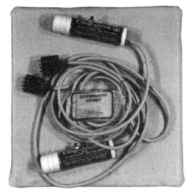

Had the president's men pulled off their burglary in secret, Watergate might have been the scandal that never happened. But everything came unstuck—because of one piece of tape.

These Chap Stick tubes fitted with tiny microphones were found in the White House safe of Watergate conspirator Howard Hunt. Possibly they were being saved for use in some future operation of the so-called White House Plumbers.

> ## " NEXT TIME THERE MAY BE NO WATCHMAN IN THE NIGHT. "
>
> —REPRESENTATIVE JAMES MANN
> OF SOUTH CAROLINA, VOTING FOR
> A BILL OF IMPEACHMENT

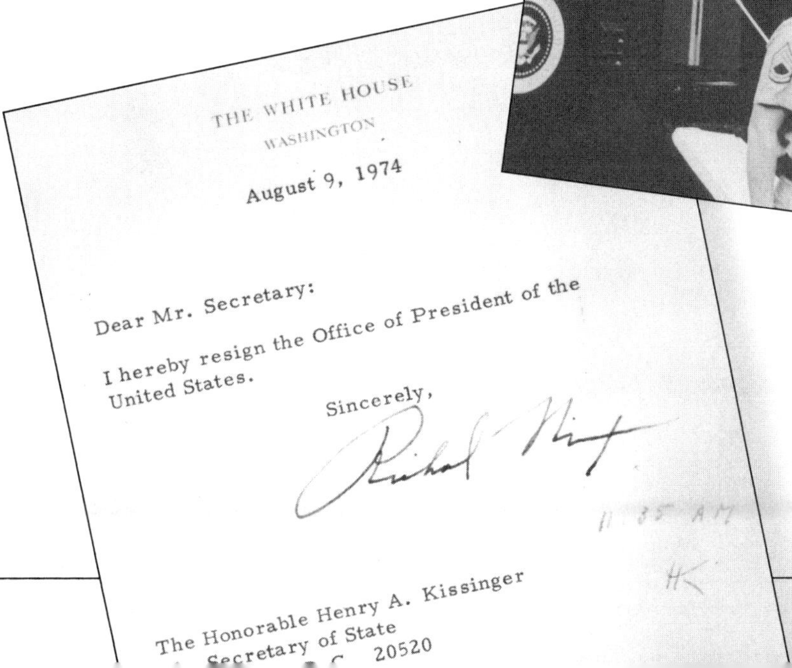

THE WHITE HOUSE
WASHINGTON

August 9, 1974

Dear Mr. Secretary:

I hereby resign the Office of President of the United States.

Sincerely,

Richard Nixon

11:35 AM

HK

The Honorable Henry A. Kissinger
Secretary of State
C 20520

WEBMASTER

Meet the man who brought the world to our fingertips.

The Internet was created by many people over many years—and yes, Al Gore did play a role. The World Wide Web, on the other hand, was the product of one man's imagination.

In 1980, software consultant Tim Berners-Lee was having trouble keeping track of all his notes. So he designed a piece of software to access everything on his computer through random links. He called it *Enquire*.

Then he got another idea: what if he could link information on many computers all over the globe? After years of thinking about this, he sat down at a computer in December of 1990, and in a few weeks created the first browser and server. "It was really not a whole lot of work," he claims.

The hard part was still to come: convincing people he was onto something. Part of that involved coming up with a name for it. Colleagues referred to it as "that hypertext thing," but Berners-Lee knew he needed something a bit more inspiring.

His first thought was to call it "the Mesh," but it sounded too much like "mess." He considered "the Information Mine," but decided that the abbreviation—TIM—sounded too egotistical. "Having people talk about finding it on the TIM would be awful," he says. Of course, he finally settled on "World Wide Web."

"It will never take off," friends told him. It did.

An early version of Berners-Lee's Web browser. He renounced patent rights on the Web to ensure its growth. Patenting it, he says, "would have scuppered the whole thing. It never would have taken off."

> **I GOT INTO A LOT OF TROUBLE WHEN SOMEBODY CALLED ME THE CREATOR OF THE WORLD WIDE WEB. I GOT AN ANGRY CALL FROM SOMEBODY WHO SAID THAT WAS PREPOSTEROUS BECAUSE I COULDN'T HAVE WRITTEN ALL THAT STUFF.**
>
> —TIM BERNERS-LEE

Berners-Lee's first program was named after Enquire Within Upon Everything— *a Victorian advice book he remembered seeing on his parents' shelves. It was in many ways the Web of its day, offering a huge mishmash of information on every topic imaginable, from preparing mutton sausages to preventing cholera, from making laxatives to using coffee as a disinfectant.*

Information is only as good as its source. I relied primarily on scholarly books, magazine articles, old newspapers, a very small number of websites that I judged to be reliable, and interviews done with people directly involved in the stories. Below are the principal sources for each of the stories—a good starting point for those interested in discovering more.

The Men Who Stole Time: *Life and Leisure in Ancient Rome* by J. P. V. D. Balsdon. *Calendar* by David Ewing Duncan.

The Olympics: Canceled: *The Complete Book of the Olympics* by David Wallechinsky. *Encyclopaedia Britannica*. "100 Years of Change" by William Oscar Johnson, *Time*, May 27, 1996.

Kidnapped: *How the Irish Saved Civilization* by Thomas Cahill. *The Catholic Encyclopedia*.

Water World: *A History of Venice* by John Norwich. *The Lion of St. Mark* by Aubrey Feist. "That Sinking Feeling, Again, as Venice's Past Haunts City's Future" by William J. Broad, *New York Times*, August 29, 2000. Gondola history courtesy of Thom Price, boatbuilder in Venice.

The Death of Attila: *Barbarians and Romans* by Justine Davis Randers-Pherson. *The Age of Attila* by C. D. Gordon. *The Huns* by E. A. Thompson.

The Man Who Didn't Discover America: *Explorers of the Americas Before Columbus* by George DeLucenay Leon. *The Viking Explorers* by Frederick J. Pohl.

Children's Crusade: *The Children's Crusade* by George Gray. *Legends, Lies and Cherished Myths of World History* by Richard Shenkman. *Brewer's Dictionary of Phrase and Fable.*

Get off the Field: *Golf: A Pictorial History* by Henry Cotton. *The Sackville Illustrated Dictionary of Golf* by Alan Booth and Michael Hobbs. "The Perfect Substitute for War" by Paul Auster, *New York Times Magazine*, April 18, 1999.

Ibn Battuta: *The Adventures of Ibn Battuta* by Ross E. Dunn. *Ibn Battuta: Travels in Asia and Africa 1325–1354*, translated and selected by H. A. R. Gibb.

Admiral Zheng's Voyages: *The Discoverers* by Daniel Boorstin. "1492 Prequel" by Nicholas Kristof, *New York Times Magazine*, June 6, 1999.

Count Vlad: *In Search of Dracula* by Raymond T. McNally and Radu Florescu.

Round, Not Flat: *The Life and Voyages of Christopher Columbus* by Washington Irving. *Lies My Teacher Told Me* by James W. Loewen.

End of an Empire: *Gold: The Fascinating Story of the Noble Metal Through the Ages* by Daniel Cohen. *The Conquest of the Incas* by John Hemming.

Disappearing Days: *Calendar* by David Ewing Duncan.

Up with Uppowoc: *They Saw It Happen*, compiled by C. R. N. Routh. *Counterblaste to Tobacco* by R.B. (King James I), published anonymously, 1604.

Coffee and the Pope: *All About Coffee* by William Ukers. *Uncommon Grounds* by Mark Prendergast.

One Sweet Deal: *The Scents of Eden* by Charles Corn. *Nathaniel's Nutmeg* by Giles Milton.

Beer and the Mayflower: *The Pilgrims in Their Three Homes* by William Eliot Griffis. *Mourt's Relation: A Journal of the Pilgrims at Plymouth*, edited by Henry Martyn. *Beer in America* by Greg Smith.

Shakespeare in Print: *By Me, William Shakespeare* by Robert Payne. *Shakespeare's England* by the editors of *Horizon*.

Tulipomania: *Tulipomania* by Mike Dash. *The Embarrassment of Riches* by Simon Schama.

Fit for a King: *A Royal Passion: Louis XIV as Patron of Architecture* by Robert Berger. *Louis XVI* by John Wolf.

The Siege That Gave Birth to the Croissant: *A History of Food* by Maguelonne Touissant-Samat. *Reader's Digest Facts and Fallacies*.

Lloyd's of London: *Uncommon Grounds* by Mark Prendergast. *Against the Odds* by Peter L. Bernstein. *Lloyd's of London* by Godfrey Hodgson.

Paper Trail: *They All Laughed* by Ira Flatow. *Get It on Paper*, THE HISTORY CHANNEL® documentary written and produced by Kate Raisz; Rick Beyer, executive producer.

English Kilt: *The Invention of Tradition,* edited by Eric Hobsbawm and Terence Ranger. "Bagpipe," *Encyclopaedia Britannica*.

From Sin to Grace: *The Atlantic Slave Trade* by David Northrup. *Amazing Grace: John Newton's Story* by John Charles Pollock. Information provided by the Cowper-Newton Museum in the United Kingdom, www.cowperandnewtonmuseum.org.

Move Over, Paul Revere: *Patriots* by A. J. Langguth. *The Lexington Alarm* by Abram Wakeman (pamphlet supplied by Connecticut Historical Society). "Unknown Patriot Outdid Revere" by Dorothy W. Chapman, *Boston Globe*, April 20, 1997. "Descendants of Israel Bissell" by Edward Church Smith et al., *American Genealogist XXVI*.

The Colonel and the Note: *Patriots* by A. J. Langguth. *The Crossing* by Howard Fast.

First President: *John Hanson, Our First President* by Seymour Weiss Smith. *The Patriot's Handbook* by George Grant.

Doctor of Death: *Guillotine* by Daniel Gerould. *Myth Information* by J. Allen Vasdi. *Citizens* by Simon Schama.

The Mechanical Internet: *The Victorian Internet* by Tom Standage. *The Early History of Data Networks* by Gerard J. Holzmann and Björn Pehrson. Author's tour of restored Chappe telegraph station in Saverne, France.

Warrior Queen: *Condemned to Repeat It* by Wick Alison. *Under the Black Flag* by David Cordingly. *Women Pirates* by Myra Weatherly.

The Real Uncle Sam: *Uncle Sam: The Man and the Legend* by Altum Ketchum. *Famous Americans You Never Knew Existed* by Bruce Felton and Mark Fowler.

Jackson and Benton: *The Revolutionary Age of Andrew Jackson* by Robert V. Remini.

"The Star-Spangled Banner": Various documents and clippings from the National Museum of American History.

Ba-Bump Goes the Stethoscope: *Great Adventures in Medicine*, edited by Samuel Rapport and Helen Wright. "The Chance Invention That Changed Medicine" by Dr. John G. Leyden, *Saturday Evening Post*, May 2001. "The Inventor of the Stethoscope: René Laënnec" by Harry Bloch, *Journal of Family Practice*, August 1993.

Night Writing: *Louis Braille* by Jennifer Fisher Bryan. *Louis Braille and Coupvray, His Birthplace* by Jean Roblin, translated by Annette Watney. *Encyclopaedia Britannica*.

First Computer: *Bit by Bit* by Stan Augarten. *The Bride of Science* by Benjamin Wooley.

In the Name of Kali: *The Stranglers* by George Ludgate Bruce. *Thugs and Dacoits of India* by James Hutton.

Family Business: *The House That Ivory Built* by the editors of *Advertising Age*. *Soap Opera: The Inside Story of Procter and Gamble* by Alecia Swasy. Boston University history professor Bruce Schulman provided information on the Panic of 1837.

One Man, One Vote: E-mail from Brad King, co–general counsel, Indiana Election Commission. *The Pioneer Era*, vol. II, by David Larmony. "The Importance of a Single Vote" by Harry S. New, *Indiana Magazine of History*, June 1935. "Edward A. Hannegan" by John Wesley Whicker, *Indiana Magazine of History*, December 1918.

Portrait of an Inventor: *The Victorian Internet* by Tom Standage. *Matthew Brady and the Image of History* by Mary Panzer. *American Leonardo* by Carlton Mahee.

The Curious Case of Phineas Gage: *The Brain* by Dr. Richard Restak. "The Amazing Case of Phineas Gage," by R. M. E. Sabbatini, www.epub.org.br.

Pin Money: *Necessity's Child* and *Famous First Facts* by Joseph Nathan Kane.

This Magic Moment: *Memoirs of Robert-Houdin* by Jean-Eugene Robert-Houdin. *A Master of Modern Magic* by Henry Ridgely Evans.

Not Whistling "Dixie": *American Popular Songs* by David Ewen. *The Civil War* by Shelby Foote. *Dan Emmett and the Rise of the Early Negro Minstrelsy* by Hans Nathan. "Daniel Decatur Emmett's Dixie" by George Bird Evans, Library of Congress.

Pony Express: *The Pony Express Goes Through* by Howard R. Dirges. Information supplied by the Pony Express Museum in Saint Joseph, Missouri.

Telephone Tale: *Sounds of Our Times* by Robert Beyer. *Philip Reis, Inventor of the Telephone* by Sylvanus Thompson. *Alexander Graham Bell: The Life and Times of the Man Who Invented the Telephone* by Edwin S. Grosvenor and Morgan Wesson. Letter from Elisha Gray to A. L. Hays, March 19, 1876, Western Union Collection, Library of Congress.

The Gun Meant to Save Lives: *American Science and Invention* by Mitchell Wilson. Various documents and clippings supplied by the Cincinnati Historical Society Library and the Connecticut State Library. "Gatling Gun" by William Bennett Edwards, *American Rifleman*, April 1990. *Encyclopaedia Britannica*.

Three Cigars: *The Civil War: Fort Sumter to Perryville* by Shelby Foote. *The Army of the Potomac: Mr. Lincoln's Army* by Bruce Catton.

Amazing Fax: *They All Laughed* by Ira Flatow. Interview with Ira Flatow, March 2001. Additional information provided by the Conservatoire National des Arts et Métiers, Paris, and the Museó Nazionale della Scienzai e della Tecnica, Milan.

The Actor and the Son: *Robert Todd Lincoln* by John S. Goff. *Abraham Lincoln* by Carl Sandburg. *Columbia Encyclopedia*.

The Beginning and the End: *Confederates in the Attic* by Tony Horwitz. *The Civil War* by Shelby Foote. *Biography of Wilmer McLean* by Frank P. Cauble.

QWERTY . . .: "The First Typewriter" by Daryl Rehr, *Popular Mechanics*, August 1996. *Get It on Paper*, THE HISTORY CHANNEL® documentary written and produced by Kate Raisz; Rick Beyer, executive producer.

Secret Subway: *Labyrinths of Iron: A History of the World's Subways* by Benson Bobrick. *Banvard's Folly* by Paul Collins. *Scientific American*, March 5, 1870, and February 4, 1912.

Not the Chicago Fire: *Fire at Peshtigo* by Robert W. Wells. *The Great Fire* by Jim Murphy. "Two Fires," *American Heritage*, October 1996.

Mrs. Satan: *The Woman Who Ran for President* by Lois Beachy Underhill. *Other Powers* by Barbara Goldsmith.

Cartoon Characters: *Ain't You Glad You Joined the Republicans* by John Calvin Batchelor. "Van Gogh, Thomas Nast and the Social Role of the Artist," by Albert Boime, *Van Gogh 100*, edited by Joseph D. Mascheck. *How It Started* by Webb Garrison.

Land War: "Captain Boycott's Crops," *Harper's Weekly*, December 1880. *Encyclopaedia Britannica; The Oxford English Dictionary*. "Charles Stewart Parnell," biography in on-line archives of the County Clare Library.

Who Killed Garfield?: *Garfield* by Allen Peskin. *Extraordinary Endings of Practically Everything* by Charles Panati. *Oops!* by Paul Kirchner. "How Did Lincoln Die" by Richard Fraser, M.D., *American Heritage*, February-March 1995.

Doctor of Reason: *Joseph Bell* by Jessie Saxby. *A Teller of Tales* by Daniel Stashower. *Dr. Joe Bell* by Ely Liebow.

Marketing the Electric Chair: *They All Laughed* by Ira Flatow. "Edison and 'The Chair'" by Terry St. Reynolds and Theodore Bernstein, *IEEE Technology and Society Magazine*, March 1989. "Critics Condemn Electric Chair," *USA Today*, September 7, 2001. Various letters and memos supplied the Edison Historical Site.

Annie and the Kaiser: *Annie Oakley* by Shirley Kasper. "The Road Not Taken: Thanks but No Cigar" by David K. Large, *Quarterly Journal of Military History*, spring 1998.

Revolution in a Cereal Bowl: *Cerealizing America* by Scott Bruce and Bill Crawford. *Good Morning*, THE HISTORY CHANNEL® documentary written and produced by Ron Blau; Rick Beyer, executive producer.

Of Flashlights and Model Trains: *All Aboard* by Ron Hollander. *American Heritage of Invention and Technology*, winter 1995.

The Election That Killed: *The Day the World Ended* by Gordon Thomas and Max Morgan Witts. *Mt. Pelée and the Tragedy of Martinique* by Angelo Heilprin. *Earthquakes and Volcanoes* by John Gribbin. "Soldiers Barred the Way to Safety," *New York Times*, May 15, 1902.

The Ice Cream Cone Cometh: "King Cone" by Richard F. Snow, *Invention and Technology*, fall 1993. "Melting Claims on First Ice Cream Cone" by Elaine Viets, *St. Louis Post-Dispatch*, June 4, 1978. Various articles supplied by the Missouri Historical Society. Interview with Linda Menches-Aleman, granddaughter of Charles Menches.

Diamond in the Rough: *The Queen's Jewels: The Personal Collection of Elizabeth II* by Leslie Field. "Inventory of the Crown Jewels Reveals Intriguing Royal History" by T. R. Reid, *Washington Post*, February 4, 1999. Cullinan & Cullinane Family Genealogy Project.

The Man Who Saved Football: *They Changed the Game* by Howard Liss. *TR: The Last Romantic* by H. W. Brands. *New York Times*, various issues in 1905 and 1906. "NCAA Born from Need to Bridge Football and Higher Education" by Kay Hawes, *NCAA News*, November 8, 1999. Archival material provided by Saint Louis University.

Eiffel, or Eyesore: *Around and About Paris* by Thirza Vallois. Website www.tour-eiffel.fr. "Eiffel Tower to Stay" *New York Times*, January 23, 1907. "Wireless to New York," *New York Times*, January 26, 1908.

America's Sport: *A.G. Spalding and the Rise of Baseball* by Peter Levine. *The Dictionary of Misinformation* by Tom Burnam.

Double O Powell: *My Adventures As a Spy* by Robert Baden-Powell. *Columbia Encyclopedia.*

Wired Wireless: "Sends 2 Programs over Light Wire," *New York Times*, May 4, 1924. Muzak Corporation archives. *Biographical Memoir of George Owen Squier* by Arthur E. Kenelly. National Academy of Sciences Archive. "Nature's Antennas" by Terence Monmany, *Science Magazine*, March 1985. "Trapped in a Musical Elevator" by Otto Friedrich, *Time*, December 10, 1984.

Wrong Turn to World War I: *Dreadnought* by Robert K. Massie. *Heroes and Legends of World War One* by Arch Whitehouse. *The Twelve Days* by George Malcolm Thomson.

The Cabdrivers Who Saved Paris: *The Guns of August* by Barbara Tuchman. *The First World War* by Martin Gilbert.

Strike Song: "National Anthem Begins the Affray," *New York Times*, September 11, 1918. *The Cultural Encyclopedia of Baseball* by Jonathan Fraser Light. *The Babe in Red Stockings* by Kerry Keene et al. Phone interview with baseball historian Robert Behn, September 1, 1998.

Forgotten Fight: *The Day They Almost Bombed Moscow* by Christopher Dobson and John Miller. *Lies My Teacher Taught Me* by James Loewen.

Carbine Williams: *Carbine* by Ross E. Beard Jr. *Patent Files*, "Carbine Williams," produced for the THE HISTORY CHANNEL® by Barbara Moran; Rick Beyer, executive producer.

Man's Best Friend: *The Great Race to Nome* by Karen Krupnick. *New York Times*, various articles, January 27–February 3, 1925.

Scopes Trial: *Summer of the Gods* by Edward J. Larsen. *Famous Trials* by Doug Lindner. Website: www.law.umkc.edu/faculty/projects/ftrials/ftrials.htm.

The Race to End All Races: *The Complete Book of the Olympics* by David Wallechinsky. "Women Athletes Collapse," *London Daily Mail*, August 3, 1928.

The Mold That Saved Millions: *In Search of Penicillin* by David Wilson. *Alexander Fleming, the Man and Myth* by Gwyn MacFarlane.

Gunfighter Golden Years: *Wyatt Earp: The Life Behind the Legend* by Casey Tefertiller. *Bat Masterson: The Man and the Legend* by Robert K. DeArment.

The Search for Planet X: *This Week in History*™, "Pluto," THE HISTORY CHANNEL®, produced by Jim DeVinney; Rick Beyer, executive producer (included interviews with various people at Lowell Observatory).

Going...Going...Gone: *The Story of Negro League Baseball* by William Brashler. *Only the Ball Was White* by Robert Person.

Don't Mess with Thanksgiving!: Clippings, letters, and memoranda on file at the Franklin D. Roosevelt Library, Hyde Park, New York.

Einstein's Error: *Einstein: A Life* by Denis Brian. *Einstein: The Life and Times* by Ronald W. Clark.

Japan's Schindler: *In Search of Sugihara* by Hillel Levine. *Japanese Diplomats and Jewish Refugees* by Pamela Rotner Sakamoto.

Live and Let Spy: *The Man Behind James Bond* by Andrew Lycett. Interview with John Pearson, Fleming's friend and biographer, March 2001.

Beautiful Brains: Interview with Anthony Loder, Hedy Lamarr's son, 2000. "Advanced Weaponry of the Stars" by Hans-Joachim Braun, *Invention and Technology*, spring 1997.

The Dead Man Who Duped Hitler: *The Man Who Never Was* by Ewen Montague. *Secret Agents, Spies and Saboteurs* by Janusz Piekalkiewics. British Public Records Office file WO 106/5921 and file ADM 223/794.

Close Call of the Porter: "Torpedo on the Starboard Beam" by Commander Charles F. Pick Jr., *Naval Institute Proceedings*, August 1970. *Affectionately, FDR* by James Roosevelt and Sidney Shalett. Log of President Roosevelt's trip aboard the USS *Iowa*, FDR Library. Author's interview with *William D. Porter* crew member Bob Jones.

The Little Boat That Won the War: *Andrew Jackson Higgins and the Boats That Won World War II* by Jerry Strahan. *D-Day* by Stephen Ambrose. *From Cotton Belt to Sunbelt* by Bruce J. Schulman.

Lost in Translation: "The Great Mokusatsu Mistake," by William J. Coughlin, *Harper's Magazine*, March 1953. *Power of Words* by Stuart Chase. *Truman* by David McCullough.

Cooking with Radar: *They All Laughed* by Ira Flatow. Raytheon Company archives. Interviews with Norm Krim and John Ossepchuk at Raytheon, June 28, 2001.

About-Face: *Presidents' Secret Wars* by John Prados. *OSS: The Secret History of America's First Central Intelligence Agency* by Richard Harris Smith.

American Pie: *Frisbee* by Stancil E. D. Johnson. *Encyclopedia of Pop Culture* by Jane and Michael Stern. "Where the Frisbee First Flew" by Jeff McDonald, www.theultimatehandbook.com. *Bridgeport: A Pictorial History* by David W. Palmquist.

A Dog's Life: "Soviet Fires New Satellite, Carrying Dog," *New York Times*, November 3, 1957. Space Today Online, www.tui.edu/STO/Astronauts/Dogs. Information from NASA archives.

A Piece of Tape: *Watergate by Fred Emery*. "5 Held in Plot to Bug Democrats' Office Here" by Alfred E. Lewis, *Washington Post*, June 18, 1972. "A Watchman Foiled Watergate Break-In" by Adam Clymer, *New York Times*, September 29, 2000.

Webmaster: Author's interview with Tim Berners-Lee, March 16, 2001.

ACKNOWLEDGMENTS

The Greatest Stories Never Told would have remained untold without the efforts of many, many people.

It began in December of 1997 with an invitation by Artie Scheff at THE HISTORY CHANNEL® to work on the project that became *Timelab 2000*® and eventually led to this book. For that alone I am grateful, but Artie has also been a source of guidance every step along the way. Thanks also to Abbe Raven, Carrie Trimmer, Cindy Berenson, and many others at THE HISTORY CHANNEL® for their assistance and support.

Many talented people assisted in finding and shaping the stories that appear here. Alison White, Melanie McLaughlin, Jim Gilmore, Richard Klug, Tom Yaroushek, Rob Stegman, Joel Olicker, Tug Yourgrau, Jen Pearce, Jim Ohm, Mike Mavretic, Barb Moran, Kate Raisz, and Bill Finnegan all deserve a share of the credit. Sam Waterston, who hosted *Timelab 2000*, constantly challenged me to be a better storyteller, and I keep trying to rise to that challenge. Patricia Barazza Vos gathered many of the images that appeared in this book and tutored me on the ins and outs of photo research so I could find the others.

Historians David Blackbourn and Steve Ozment, from Harvard, and Bruce Schulman and Jill Lepore, from Boston University, consulted on the project, steering me away from many problem stories. I hasten to add that any remaining inaccuracies are mine, not theirs.

I would like to thank the librarians at the Cary Memorial Library in Lexington, Massachusetts, for their assistance and their patience. With their help—and the interlibrary loan system operated by the Minuteman Library Network—I was able to get my hands on books from all over the country. I also owe a debt of thanks to librarians at the U.S. National Archives, the FDR Library, the Burndy Library at MIT, the Library of Congress, and elsewhere who assisted in my research efforts.

It is with my tongue only somewhat in my cheek that I thank Tim Berners-Lee for inventing the World Wide Web, without which I never could have tracked down all the photos that appear here. Tim was also kind enough to submit to an interview, on which the last story in the book is based.

My business partners, Mark Tomizawa, Linda Button, and Marilyn Kass, have all been unstinting in their support, for reasons that escape me but for which I am very appreciative.

It takes an army of talented people to turn a manuscript into a book. Thanks to Gene Mackles, who developed the initial visual concept; Leah Carlson-Stanisic, for her expert art direction; Judith Stagnitto Abbate, who designed the interior and laid out the pages; copy editor Chuck Antony, whose proofreading and fact checking were invaluable; Mucca Design, who designed the cover; production editor Diane Aronson; and of course, Joelle Yudin, always there to answer my questions, no matter how inane they might have seemed.

Arielle Eckstut, my agent, believed in the idea of this book from the beginning and guided me through the process of writing my first book with a steady hand and a ready supply of enthusiasm. There simply wouldn't be a book without her. Similarly, my editor, Mauro Dipreta, has been a great champion of the book as we navigated the production process, and for that I am extremely grateful.

My children, Roberta and Andrew, have shown great tolerance toward a dad who has disappeared into his office on many a night and weekend to slave away on "the book." They have also worked on it themselves, proofreading, scanning, xeroxing, and offering some very astute suggestions.

Finally, my wife, Marilyn, has been an unending source of support and inspiration. Her red pencil has traveled these pages and made them better. She has lifted me up in my darkest hours and never hesitates to bring me down to earth when I get a little full of myself. For that, and for so many other things, I owe her a debt I never can repay.

All credits listed by page number, top to bottom. Photos are generally credited only the first time they appear.

Every effort has been made to correctly attribute all the materials reproduced in this book. If any errors have been made, we will be happy to correct them in future editions.

Page x: ©Araldo De Luca/CORBIS; Library of Congress. **Page 1:** Library of Congress (all). **Page 2:** ©Bettmann/CORBIS. **Page 3:** Library of Congress; Getty Images. **Page 5:** Library of Congress; ©CORBIS; Planet Art. **Page 7:** Collection of author; Library of Congress (bottom two). **Page 8:** Planet Art; ©Hulton-Deutsch Collection/CORBIS. **Page 9:** ©Bettmann/CORBIS. **Page 10:** ©Bettmann/CORBIS; D.W. Roth. **Page 11:** Stofnun Arna Magnussonar. **Pages 12-13:** ©Bettmann/CORBIS (all.). **Pages 14-15:** Mary Evans Picture Library (all). **Page 17:** Library of Congress; Illustration by author; ©CORBIS. **Page 19:** Illustration by Dugald Stermer/Courtesy *The New York Times* (top and bottom); ©Philadelphia Museum of Art/CORBIS. **Page 21:** Collection of author; Stock Montage/Getty Images. **Page 22:** ©Bettmann/CORBIS. **Page 23:** Library of Congress. **Pages 24-25:** Library of Congress (all). **Page 26:** ©Bettmann/CORBIS. **Page 27:** ©Archivo Iconografico, S.A./CORBIS. **Page 28:** Collection of author; The Huntington Library, San Marino, California. **Page 29:** Library of Congress, The Huntington Library, San Marino, California. **Page 30:** ©Bettmann/CORBIS; Digital Stock. **Page 31:** ©Bettmann/CORBIS; ©Leonard de Selva/CORBIS. **Page 32:** Library of Congress. **Page 33:** ©Abbie Enock; Travel Ink/CORBIS; Library of Congress. **Page 34:** Library of Congress; Collection of author. **Page 35:** Hulton|Archive by Getty Images (top and bottom). **Page 36:** Library of

Congress; Library of Congress. **Page 37:** Library of Congress (top and bottom); Schoenberg Center for Electronic Text & Image, University of Pennsylvania Library. **Page 38:** Hulton|Archive by Getty Images; PictureQuest/CORBIS. **Page 39:** Library of Congress; Library of Congress. **Page 40:** Library of Congress; ©Yann Arthus-Bertrand/CORBIS. **Page 41:** Library of Congress (bottom). **Page 42:** ©Archivo Iconografico, S.A./CORBIS; Picture Quest/Burke/Triolo. **Page 43:** Library of Congress. **Page 44:** Lloyd's of London; ©Bettmann/CORBIS. **Page 45:** Lloyd's of London (all). **Page 46:** The Burndy Library, Dibner Institute for the History of Science and Technology, Cambridge, Massachusetts. **Page 47:** Collection of author; Elaine Koretsky; Crane & Co. Inc. **Pages 48-49:** ©Bettmann/CORBIS (all except lower right); ©AFP/CORBIS. **Page 50:** Library of Congress (all). **Page 51:** Library of Congress (top and bottom); Cowper and Newton Museum. **Page 52:** Collection of author (both). **Page 53:** Collection of the author; The Connecticut Historical Society, Hartford, Connecticut; The Historical Society of Pennsylvania. **Page 55:** Library of Congress (top and bottom); Etching by Arthur Szyk reproduced with permission of Alexandra Szyk Bracie and The Arthur Szyk Society, www.syzk.org. **Page 56:** National Archives; Library of Congress. **Page 57:** National Archives. **Pages 58-59:** ©Bettmann/CORBIS (all). **Pages 60-61:** The Burndy Library, Dibner Institute for the History of Science and Technology, Cambridge, Massachusetts (all except lower left); Societe d'Histoire de la Poste et de France Telecom en Alsace. **Pages 62-63:** Collection of author (all). **Page 64:** National Archives. **Page 65:** Sketch by William Gropper from Library of Congress and used by permission of Craig Gropper. **Pages 66-67:** Library of Congress (all). **Page 69:** American Antiquarian Society; Library of Congress. **Page 70:** ©Bettmann/CORBIS; Collection of author. **Page 71:** The Warren Anatomical Museum, Francis A. Countway Library of Medicine, Harvard Medical School. **Pages 72-73:** Maison Natale de Louis Braille, Coupvray, France (all except upper left); Library of Congress. **Page 74:** ©Bettmann/CORBIS; Library of Congress. **Page 75:** Bettmann/CORBIS (top and bottom); Schoenberg Center for Electronic Text & Image, University of Pennsylvania Library. **Page 76:** Collection of author; ©Arvind Garg/CORBIS. **Pages 78-79:** Procter and Gamble (all except lower right); Collection of author. **Pages 80-81:** Library of Congress (all). **Page 82:** U.S. Patent and Trademark Office; Smithsonian Institution. **Page 83:** Library of Congress (top two); City of New York. **Page 85:** Library of Congress; The Warren Anatomical Museum, Francis A. Countway Library of Medicine, Harvard Medical School; H. Damasio, T. Grabowski, R. Frank, A. M. Galaburda, A. R. Damasio: "The return of Phineas Gage: Clues about the brain from a famous patient." *Science*, 246:1102-1105, 1994. Department of Neurology and Image Analysis Facility, University of Iowa. **Page 87:** U.S. Patent and Trademark Office; National Museum of American History, Smithsonian Institution. **Pages 88-89:** Library of Congress (all). **Page 90:** Library of Congress (all). **Page 91:** Rare Book, Manuscript, & Special Collections Library, Duke University (top two images). Page 92: ©Bettmann/CORBIS. **Page 93:** Library of Congress; National Archives. **Page 95:** Heimatmuseum Gelnhausen; National Archives; Library of Congress. **Page 97:** Colt Collection, Connecticut State Library (all except "Camel" gun); Library of Congress. **Pages 98-99:**

Library of Congress (all). **Page 100:** International Telecommunication Union Telecommunication Journal (ITUVJ); Archivo fotografico del Museo Nazionale della Scienza e della Tecnologia di Milano, Italia. **Page 101:** ITUVJ (top and bottom); Collection of author. **Pages 102-103:** Library of Congress (all). **Page 104:** National Archives; Library of Congress. **Page 106:** Daryl Rehr (all). **Page 107:** U. S. Patent and Trademark Office; Wisconsin Historial Society, Whi-3218; Daryl Rehr. **Page 109:** Collection of author (top and bottom); Museum of the City of New York. **Page 111:** Wisconsin Historical Society, Whi-1784; Collection of author. **Page 112:** Library of Congress; Robin Holland-Martin. **Page 113:** Collection of author; Library of Congress. **Pages 114-115:** Library of Congress (all except Santa); ©Bettmann/CORBIS. **Page 117:** Library of Congress; ©Sean Sexton Collection/CORBIS; Collection of author. **Page 118:** Culver Pictures; National Museum of Health and Medicine. **Page 119:** Collection of author; Culver Pictures. **Page 120:** Collection of author; ©Historical Picture Archive/CORBIS. **Page 121:** ©Historical Picture Archive/CORBIS (top and bottom); Collection of author. **Page 122:** ©CORBIS; National Park Service. **Page 123:** Collection of author (top and bottom); ©CORBIS. **Page 124:** Library of Congress; National Archives. **Page 125:** National Archives (top and bottom); Library of Congress. **Page 126:** Library of Congress; W. K. Kellogg Foundation. **Page 127:** Kellogg Company; Archives and Special Collections, Del E. Webb Memorial Library, Loma Linda University, Loma Linda, California. **Page 128:** Lionel; Collection of author. **Page 129:** U.S. Patent and Trademark Office; Lionel; Lionel. **Pages 130-131:** Library of Congress (all except lower left); Collection of author. **Page 133:** Illustration by D.W. Roth; Monty Lyon Collection, Missouri Historical Society, Saint Louis; Menches Brothers. **Page 134:** Crown Copyright: Historic Royal Palaces. **Page 135:** ©Hulton-Deutsch Collection/CORBIS; Library of Congress. **Page 136:** Library of Congress; Collection of author. **Page 137:** Yale University Library (top and bottom); Saint Louis University Archives. **Pages 138-139:** Library of Congress (all except headline); Collection of author. **Page 140:** Library of Congress; National Archives. **Page 141:** Library of Congress (top two); National Baseball Hall of Fame Library, Cooperstown, N.Y. **Page 142-143:** Library of Congress (all except butterfly sketches); Collection of author. **Page 144:** Muzak LLC (all). **Page 145:** National Archives; Muzak LLC (bottom two). **Page 147:** ©Bettmann/CORBIS (top and bottom); TIMEPIX. **Page 149:** National Archives; Renault; Library of Congress. **Page 150:** Reprinted courtesy of the Boston Globe; Collection of author. **Page 151:** Library of Congress. **Pages 152-153:** Library of Congress (all). **Page 155:** U.S. Patent and Trademark office; Williams family; Williams family. **Page 156:** ©Underwood & Underwood/CORBIS; Illustration by author. **Page 157:** ©Bettmann/CORBIS. **Page 159:** Library of Congress; ©Underwood & Underwood/CORBIS. **Page 161:** Library of Congress, ©IOC/Olympic Museum Archives; Collection of author (bottom two). **Page 163:** Library of Congress; Library of Congress; Hulton|Archive by Getty Images. **Page 164:** National Archives. **Page 165:** Colt Collection, Connecticut State Library; Library of Congress; Brown Brothers. **Pages 166-167:** © by Lowell Observatory, Used by Permission (all). **Pages 168-169:** National Baseball Hall of Fame Library, Cooperstown, N.Y. (all photos except portrait of

Gibson); ©Bettmann/CORBIS. **Pages 170-171:** Franklin D. Roosevelt Library and Museum (all). **Page 173:** National Archives; TIMEPIX. **Page 175:** Collection of Susan Bluman (top and bottom); JCC Tokyo. **Page 177:** Library of Congress; ©Bettmann/CORBIS; ©Hulton-Deutsch Collection/CORBIS; Cover from *A Field Guide To Birds of The West Indies* (Boston: Houghton Mifflin, 1999). **Page 178:** Frames from Extase courtesy Video Dimensions. **Page 179:** American Heritage of Invention and Technology/Photo: Kobal Collection; Anthony Loder. **Pages 180-181:** Public Record Office, WO 106/5921 (all). **Page 183:** Franklin D. Roosevelt Library and Museum; National Archives; National Archives. **Page 184:** Franklin D. Roosevelt Library and Museum; Jerrry Strahan/Higgins family. **Page 185:** Jerry Strahan/Higgins family. **Page 186:** Harry S. Truman Library and Museum; National Archives. **Page 187:** Harry S. Truman Library and Museum; National Archives. **Pages 188-189:** Raytheon Company (all). **Page 190:** TIMEPIX. **Page 191:** National Archives (top and bottom); R. Harriss Smith. **Page 192:** Collection of author. **Page 193:** U.S. Patent and Trademark Office; ©2002 Wham-O Inc. All Rights Reserved; Connecticut State Library. **Page 194:** Library of Congress; NASA. **Page 195:** Library of Congress (top and bottom); ©Bettmann/CORBIS. **Pages 196-197:** National Archives (all). **Page 199:** World Wide Web Consortium; Collection of author; ©Henry Horenstein/CORBIS.

(Credit for pages not listed can be found in the credits for the facing page.)